A TALE OF

Charles Dickens

AUTHORED by Eleanor Campisano
UPDATED AND REVISED by Michelle Rosenberg

COVER DESIGN by Table XI Partners LLC
COVER PHOTO by Olivia Verma and © 2005 GradeSaver, LLC

BOOK DESIGN by Table XI Partners LLC

Published by GradeSaver LLC, www.gradesaver.com

First published in the United States of America by GradeSaver LLC. 2015

GRADESAVER, the GradeSaver logo and the phrase "Getting you the grade since 1999" are registered trademarks of GradeSaver, LLC

ISBN 978-1-60259-635-1

Printed in the United States of America

For other products and additional information please visit http://www.gradesaver.com

Table of Contents

Biography of Charles Dickens (1812–1870)

Charles Dickens was born in Portsmouth, England, on February 7, 1812, to John and Elizabeth Dickens. He was the second of eight children. His mother had been in service to Lord Crew, and his father worked as a clerk for the Naval Pay office. John Dickens was imprisoned for debt when Charles was young. Charles Dickens went to work at a blacking warehouse, managed by a relative of his mother, when he was twelve, and his brush with hard times and poverty affected him deeply. He later recounted these experiences in the semi-autobiographical novel David Copperfield. Similarly, the concern for social justice and reform which surfaced later in his writings grew out of the harsh conditions he experienced in the warehouse.

As a young boy, Charles Dickens was exposed to many artistic and literary works that allowed his imagination to grow and develop considerably. He was greatly influenced by the stories his nursemaid used to tell him and by his many visits to the theater. Additionally, Dickens loved to read. Among his favorite works were *Don Quixote* by Miguel de Cervantes, *Tom Jones* by Henry Fielding, and *Arabian Nights*, all of which were picaresque novels composed of a series of loosely linked adventures. This format no doubt played a part in Dickens' idea to serialize his future works.

Dickens was able to leave the blacking factory after his father's release from prison, and he continued his education at the Wellington House Academy. Although he had little formal schooling, Dickens was able to teach himself shorthand and launch a career as a journalist. At the age of sixteen, Dickens got himself a job as a court reporter, and shortly thereafter he joined the staff of *A Mirror of Parliament*, a newspaper that reported on the decisions of Parliament. During this time Charles continued to read voraciously at the British Library, and he experimented with acting and stage-managing amateur theatricals. His experience acting would affect his work throughout his life--he was known to act out characters he was writing in the mirror and then describe himself as the character in prose in his novels.

Fast becoming disillusioned with politics, Dickens developed an interest in social reform and began contributing to the *True Sun*, a radical newspaper. Although his main avenue of work would consist of writing novels, Dickens continued his journalistic work until the end of his life, editing *The Daily News*, *Household Words*, and *All the Year Round*. His connections to various magazines and newspapers as a political journalist gave him the opportunity to begin publishing his own fiction at the beginning of his career. He would go on to write fifteen novels. (A final one, *The Mystery of Edwin Drood*, was left unfinished upon his death.)

While he published several sketches in magazines, it was not until he serialized *The Pickwick Papers* over 1836-37 that he experienced true success. A publishing phenomenon, *The Pickwick Papers* was published in monthly installments and sold over forty thousand copies of each issue. Dickens was the first person to make this serialization of novels profitable and was able to expand his audience to include those who could not normally afford such literary works.

Within a few years, he was regarded as one of the most successful authors of his time, with approximately one out of every ten people in Victorian England avidly reading and following his writings. In 1836 Dickens also married Catherine Hogarth, the daughter of a fellow co-worker at his newspaper. The couple had ten children before their separation in 1858.

Oliver Twist and *Nicholas Nickleby* followed in monthly installments, and both reflected Dickens' understanding of the lower classes as well as his comic genius. In 1843, Dickens published one of his most famous works, *A Christmas Carol*. His disenchantment with the world's economic drives is clear in this work; he blames much of society's ills on people's obsession with earning money and acquiring status based on money.

His travels abroad in the 1840s, first to America and then through Europe, marked the beginning of a new stage in Dickens' life. His writings became longer and more serious. In *David Copperfield* (1849-50), readers find the same flawed world that Dickens discovered as a young boy. Dickens published some of his best-known novels including *A Tale of Two Cities* and *Great Expectations* in his own weekly periodicals.

The inspiration to write a novel set during the French Revolution came from Dickens' faithful annual habit of reading Thomas Carlyle's book *The French Revolution*, first published in 1839. When Dickens acted in Wilkie Collins' play *The Frozen Deep* in 1857, he was inspired by his own role as a self-sacrificing lover. He eventually decided to place his own sacrificing lover in the revolutionary period, a period of great social upheaval. A year later, Dickens went through his own form of social change as he was writing *A Tale of Two Cities*: he separated from his wife, and he revitalized his career by making plans for a new weekly literary journal called *All the Year Round*. In 1859, *A Tale of Two Cities* premiered in parts in this journal. Its popularity was based not only on the fame of its author, but also on its short length and radical (for Dickens' time) subject matter.

Dickens' health began to deteriorate in the 1860s. In 1858, in response to his increasing fame, he had begun public readings of his works. These exacted a great physical toll on him. An immensely profitable but physically shattering series of readings in America in 1867-68 sped his decline, and he collapsed during a "farewell" series in England.

On June 9, 1870, Charles Dickens died. He was buried in Poet's Corner of Westminster Abbey. Though he left *The Mystery of Edwin Drood* unfinished, he had already written fifteen substantial novels and countless shorter pieces. His legacy is clear. In a whimsical and unique fashion, Dickens pointed out society's flaws in terms of its blinding greed for money and its neglect of the lower classes of society. Through his books, we come to understand the virtues of a loving heart and the pleasures of home in a flawed, cruelly indifferent world. Among English writers, in terms of his fame and of the public's recognition of his characters and stories, he is second only to William Shakespeare.

Biography of Charles Dickens (1812–1870)

Teacher Guide - About the Author

Charles Dickens was born in Portsmouth, England, on February 7, 1812, to John and Elizabeth Dickens. He was the second of eight children. His mother had been in service to Lord Crew, and his father worked as a clerk for the Naval Pay office. John Dickens was imprisoned for debt when Charles was young. Charles Dickens went to work at a blacking warehouse, managed by a relative of his mother, when he was twelve, and his brush with hard times and poverty affected him deeply. He later recounted these experiences in the semi-autobiographical novel _David Copperfield_. Similarly, the concern for social justice and reform which surfaced later in his writings grew out of the harsh conditions he experienced in the warehouse.

As a young boy, Charles Dickens was exposed to many artistic and literary works that allowed his imagination to grow and develop considerably. He was greatly influenced by the stories his nursemaid used to tell him and by his many visits to the theater. Additionally, Dickens loved to read. Among his favorite works were _Don Quixote_ by Miguel de Cervantes, _Tom Jones_ by Henry Fielding, and _Arabian Nights_, all of which were picaresque novels composed of a series of loosely linked adventures. This format no doubt played a part in Dickens' idea to serialize his future works.

Dickens was able to leave the blacking factory after his father's release from prison, and he continued his education at the Wellington House Academy. Although he had little formal schooling, Dickens was able to teach himself shorthand and launch a career as a journalist. At the age of sixteen, Dickens got himself a job as a court reporter, and shortly thereafter he joined the staff of _A Mirror of Parliament_, a newspaper that reported on the decisions of Parliament. During this time Charles continued to read voraciously at the British Library, and he experimented with acting and stage-managing amateur theatricals. His experience acting would affect his work throughout his life--he was known to act out characters he was writing in the mirror and then describe himself as the character in prose in his novels.

Fast becoming disillusioned with politics, Dickens developed an interest in social reform and began contributing to the _True Sun_, a radical newspaper. Although his main avenue of work would consist of writing novels, Dickens continued his journalistic work until the end of his life, editing _The Daily News_, _Household Words_, and _All the Year Round_. His connections to various magazines and newspapers as a political journalist gave him the opportunity to begin publishing his own fiction at the beginning of his career. He would go on to write fifteen novels. (A final one, _The Mystery of Edwin Drood_, was left unfinished upon his death.)

While he published several sketches in magazines, it was not until he serialized _The Pickwick Papers_ over 1836-37 that he experienced true success. A publishing phenomenon, _The Pickwick Papers_ was published in monthly installments and sold over forty thousand copies of each issue. Dickens was the first person to make this serialization of novels profitable and was able to expand his audience to include those who could not normally afford such literary works.

Within a few years, he was regarded as one of the most successful authors of his time, with approximately one out of every ten people in Victorian England avidly reading and following his writings. In 1836 Dickens also married Catherine Hogarth, the daughter of a fellow co-worker at his newspaper. The couple had ten children before their separation in 1858.

Oliver Twist and _Nicholas Nickleby_ followed in monthly installments, and both reflected Dickens' understanding of the lower classes as well as his comic genius. In 1843, Dickens published one of his most famous works, _A Christmas Carol_. His disenchantment with the world's economic drives is clear in this work; he blames much of society's ills on people's obsession with earning money and acquiring status based on money.

His travels abroad in the 1840s, first to America and then through Europe, marked the beginning of a new stage in Dickens' life. His writings became longer and more serious. In _David Copperfield_ (1849-50), readers find the same flawed world that Dickens discovered as a young boy. Dickens published some of his best-known novels including _A Tale of Two Cities_ and _Great Expectations_ in his own weekly periodicals.

The inspiration to write a novel set during the French Revolution came from Dickens' faithful annual habit of reading Thomas Carlyle's book _The French Revolution_, first published in 1839. When Dickens acted in Wilkie Collins' play _The Frozen Deep_ in 1857, he was inspired by his own role as a self-sacrificing lover. He eventually decided to place his own sacrificing lover in the revolutionary period, a period of great social upheaval. A year later, Dickens went through his own form of social change as he was writing _A Tale of Two Cities_: he separated from his wife, and he revitalized his career by making plans for a new weekly literary journal called _All the Year Round_. In 1859, _A Tale of Two Cities_ premiered in parts in this journal. Its popularity was based not only on the fame of its author, but also on its short length and radical (for Dickens' time) subject matter.

Dickens' health began to deteriorate in the 1860s. In 1858, in response to his increasing fame, he had begun public readings of his works. These exacted a great physical toll on him. An immensely profitable but physically shattering series of readings in America in 1867-68 sped his decline, and he collapsed during a "farewell" series in England.

On June 9, 1870, Charles Dickens died. He was buried in Poet's Corner of Westminster Abbey. Though he left _The Mystery of Edwin Drood_ unfinished, he had already written fifteen substantial novels and countless shorter pieces. His legacy is clear. In a whimsical and unique fashion, Dickens pointed out society's flaws in terms of its blinding greed for money and its neglect of the lower classes of society. Through his books, we come to understand the virtues of a loving heart and the pleasures of home in a flawed, cruelly indifferent world. Among English writers, in terms of his fame and of the public's recognition of his characters and stories, he is second only to William Shakespeare.

Teacher Guide - Study Objectives

If all of the elements of this lesson plan are employed, students will develop the following powers, skills, and understanding:

1. Students will be able to understand the elements of Charles Dickens's life and experiences that shaped his worldview and his writings.

2. Students will be able to analyze the historical and cultural framing for the novel.

3. Students will be able to read *A Tale of Two Cities* with an eye to the linguistic and thematic details that mark Dickens's style.

4. Students will be able to analyze and discuss, both individually and as a class, the notable ideas and important themes in *A Tale of Two Cities*.

5. Students will be able to evaluate the historical and cultural impact of *A Tale of Two Cities* on later literary works.

6. Students will be able to speak and write with insight about the literary themes and cultural messages in *A Tale of Two Cities*, demonstrating an ability to make a clear and articulate argument supported by textual evidence, in both verbal discussions and written form.

Teacher Guide - Common Core Standards

1. 11-12

   CCSS.ELA-Literacy.CCRA.R.1 Read closely to determine what the text says explicitly and to make logical inferences from it; cite specific textual evidence when writing or speaking to support conclusions drawn from the text.

2. 11-12

   CCSS.ELA-Literacy.CCRA.R.2 Determine central ideas or themes of a text and analyze their development; summarize the key supporting details and ideas.

3. 11-12

   CCSS.ELA-Literacy.CCRA.R.3 Analyze how and why individuals, events, or ideas develop and interact over the course of a text.

4. 11-12

   CCSS.ELA-Literacy.CCRA.R.4 Interpret words and phrases as they are used in a text, including determining technical, connotative, and figurative meanings, and analyze how specific word choices shape meaning or tone.

5. 11-12

   CCSS.ELA-Literacy.CCRA.R.5 Analyze the structure of texts, including how specific sentences, paragraphs, and larger portions of the text (e.g., a section, chapter, scene, or stanza) relate to each other and the whole.

6. 11-12

   CCSS.ELA-Literacy.CCRA.R.6 Assess how point of view or purpose shapes the content and style of a text.

7. 11-12

   CCSS.ELA-Literacy.CCRA.R.7 Integrate and evaluate content presented in diverse media and formats, including visually and quantitatively, as well as in words.

8. 11-12

CCSS.ELA-Literacy.CCRA.R.9 Analyze how two or more texts address similar themes or topics in order to build knowledge or to compare the approaches the authors take.

9. 11-12

CCSS.ELA-Literacy.CCRA.R.10 Read and comprehend complex literary and informational texts independently and proficiently.

10. 11-12

CCSS.ELA-Literacy.CCRA.W.2 Write informative/explanatory texts to examine and convey complex ideas and information clearly and accurately through the effective selection, organization, and analysis of content.

11. 11-12

CCSS.ELA-Literacy.CCRA.W.3 Write narratives to develop real or imagined experiences or events using effective technique, well-chosen details and well-structured event sequences.

12. 11-12

CCSS.ELA-Literacy.CCRA.W.6 Use technology, including the Internet, to produce and publish writing and to interact and collaborate with others.

13. 11-12

CCSS.ELA-Literacy.CCRA.W.7 Conduct short as well as more sustained research projects based on focused questions, demonstrating understanding of the subject under investigation.

14. 11-12

CCSS.ELA-Literacy.CCRA.W.8 Gather relevant information from multiple print and digital sources, assess the credibility and accuracy of each source, and integrate the information while avoiding plagiarism.

15. 11-12

CCSS.ELA-Literacy.CCRA.SL.1 Prepare for and participate effectively in a range of conversations and collaborations with diverse partners, building on others' ideas and expressing their own clearly and persuasively.

16. 11-12

CCSS.ELA-Literacy.CCRA.SL.4 Present information, findings, and supporting evidence such that listeners can follow the line of reasoning and the organization, development, and style are appropriate to task, purpose, and audience.

17. 11-12

CCSS.ELA-Literacy.CCRA.SL.5 Make strategic use of digital media and visual displays of data to express information and enhance understanding of presentations.

18. 11-12

CCSS.ELA-Literacy.CCRA.SL.6 Adapt speech to a variety of contexts and communicative tasks, demonstrating command of formal English when indicated or appropriate.

19. 11-12

CCSS.ELA-Literacy.CCRA.L.5 Demonstrate understanding of figurative language, word relationships, and nuances in word meanings.

Teacher Guide - Introduction to A Tale of Two Cities

A Tale of Two Cities, Charles Dickens's twelfth novel, was published serially in weekly installments in Dickens's own literary journal, *All the Year Round*, beginning in April of 1859. As Dickens mentions in the Preface of the novel, he came up with the basic concept while playing a self-sacrificing, heroic protagonist in a production of Wilkie Collins's play The *Frozen Deep*, which he put on with his family and friends. Expanding the concept of noble self-sacrifice to a broader narrative context, Dickens modeled Sydney Carton after Collins's protagonist and placed his story in the time period just around the French Revolution. Wanting to ensure historical accuracy, Dickens relied heavily on Thomas Carlyle's renowned history of the French Revolution to inform his writing.

As a partially historically-based novel, *A Tale of Two Cities* is unique among Dickens's novels. In the only other Dickens novel that deals with actual history as a component of the story, *Barnaby Rudge*, the historical events in question (the Gordon Riots in England) are only a minor element of the plot. In order to illuminate the historical context of the novel for his readers, Dickens talks at length about the French Revolution in *A Tale of Two Cities*. As a result, readers who are used to other Dickens novels that focus primarily on in-depth character development and witty social commentary are often surprised by the historical and political focus of *A Tale of Two Cities*.

The French Revolution began in 1789 and was characterized by the lower classes rising up en masse against the aristocracy and royalty, and successfully toppling the oppressive regime. Although many of the initial motivations behind the Revolution were admirable, as the Revolution raged on, the intentional nature of the revolutionaries' goals devolved into bloodthirsty terror. Indeed, the guillotine was used to behead Queen Marie Antoinette and impoverished peasants alike--anyone who the leading revolutionaries deemed a threat to their goals. Initially, many radicals in England supported the Revolution, which garnered backlash from Conservatives such as Edmund Burke, author of the damning commentary on the Revolution, *Reflections on the Revolution in France*. As the revolutionary movement devolved into prolonged chaos and increasingly indiscriminate bloodshed, the Revolution lost much of its support in England, so did not inspire a similar movement there.

For Dickens, the French Revolution brought up many challenging issues, as he was a staunch political progressive himself who advocated for radical reforms of poor laws of the era and significant changes to England's approach to social inequity. *A Tale of Two Cities* demonstrates Dickens's conflicting feelings about the Revolution. He writes in great depth and detail about the poverty and oppression the French peasants suffered and vividly illustrates the callous barbarity of the aristocracy, suggesting that he understands the revolutionaries' motivations. At the same time, Dickens also unsparingly portrays the brutality of the revolutionaries' methods as they gain power and influence.

Interestingly, Dickens built *A Tale of Two Cities* around the stable romance and unfailing marriage between Charles Darnay and Lucie Manette--all while his own personal life was falling into disarray. For many years, Dickens had been locked in an unhappy union with Catherine Hogarth. But while he was acting in Wilkie Collins's play--incidentally, the inspiration for the seed idea of the novel--Dickens met and fell in love with a young actress named Ellen Ternan. His relationship with Ternan was the final nail in the coffin of his troubled marriage, causing him to his separation from Hogarth in 1859. Divorce, a rare occurrence at the time, was unsurprisingly strongly frowned upon in Victorian England. As a result, this highly publicized turn of events in Dickens's personal life, along with several subsequent affairs, which also garnered significant media attention, marred the famous author's previously wholesome reputation and towards the end of his life.

Key Aspects of A Tale of Two Cities

Tone

The tone varies throughout the novel, ranging from compassionate and sentimental to alarmed, gory, and dark. In addition, there are portions of the novel written with Dickens's characteristic wit and sarcasm.

Setting

The novel takes places in 1775 through 1793, with events taking place in both London and Paris, as well as the two cities immediate surrounding areas.

Point of view

Although the third person, omniscient narrator remains anonymous throughout the novel, the reader can think of him as Dickens himself. The narrator switches focus frequently between different cities and characters, revealing historical events and context, as well as characters' inner thoughts, ideas, motivations, and emotions throughout the novel.

Character development

Sydney Carton

Although he seems unassuming at first, Sydney Carton becomes one of the most surprising and dynamic characters in the novel. At the beginning of the novel, Carton is a London attorney who began his career with great potential, but has since devolved into a life of laziness, alcoholism, and vice. He believes his life is a waste and regularly makes a point to say that he does not truly care for anyone or anything. Yet despite his apparent apathy, the reader senses that Carton actually subconsciously longs for a greater sense of purpose and meaning in his life. Even early on in the novel, just after Carton has helped to rescue Charles Darnay from conviction and execution, Carton cynical and sarcastic comments about Lucie show both his bitter personal biases as well as revealing his secret, developing feelings for Lucie Manette. Over time, however, Carton comes to recognize his attraction towards Miss Manette. Although he initially dismisses his romantic feelings as completely unrealistic, he is eventually able to profess his love to her directly. Not surprisingly, Lucie goes on to marry Darnay anyway, and Carton persists in believing himself to be a worthless human being, but this scene marks a turning point in Carton's life.

Carton's ultimate sacrifice at the end of the novel--going to the guillotine in Darnay's place--has proven controversial for many readers and critics ever since *A Tale of Two Cities* was written. Some critics argue that this is the unavoidable (and unsurprising) conclusion of a novel that focuses so heavily on themes of sacrifice, redemption, and resurrection. In this reading of the story, Carton's sacrifice of his own life mimics Christ's sacrifice for humanity, giving new life to Charles Darnay through his own death. Dickens provides further reinforcement for this interpretation of the story through his frequent use of imagery generally associated with Jesus's crucifixion and resurrection, for example the references to wine and blood throughout the novel. Despite this symbolism and thematic repetition, other critics and readers argue that Carton's sacrifice is not necessarily all that meaningful, since he did not place a lot of value on his life in the first place. Although some readers may not see Carton's life and death as very significant, Dickens seems to suggest that Carton's self-sacrifice is a necessary part of giving his life meaning and purpose.

Doctor Manette

Doctor Manette takes on an interesting role in *A Tale of Two Cities*, as Dickens uses him to convey one of the overarching ideas about the world and humanity--that the way Fate impacts each of us is a mystery. For example, throughout much of the novel, the reader does not know the reason behind Doctor Manette's original incarceration in the Bastille for eighteen years. Even when the story about his relationship with the Evrémonde family is revealed, we still never learn much about what he experienced in prison for those many years. All that the reader gets to see is the impact of his imprisonment and the implications of the tremendous suffering he must have endured, suggested by his obsessive focus on his shoemaking habit as a coping mechanism.

Despite all he has experienced, however, Manette experiences a massive transformation over the course of the novel. He begins the novel as a broken man who has been thoroughly traumatized by his lengthy imprisonment. After his release from jail, the meaningful experiences and loving relationships that Manette enjoys over the course of the novel strengthen him and bring him (figuratively) back to life. Although this transformation of Manette's character, caused by the experiences and relationships in his life, may not seem all that notable to modern readers, the idea

Dickens suggests through this change--that people's surroundings and experiences can impact their lives and identities--was actually quite revolutionary in his time. In addition, Manette's ability to transform himself from damaged former prisoner into strong and dedicated family patriarch reinforces the theme of Resurrection that permeates the novel. Furthermore, Manette's experiences over the course of the story further confirm Sydney Carton's realization that the worth of his life can be determined by his positive impact on others.

Madame Defarge

In many ways, Madame Defarge serves as both a character in her own right and a symbol for the broader motivations behind the Revolution. Early in the novel, Defarge seems mild and unthreatening, simply knitting quietly in the wine-shop. However, the reader soon learns that Defarge is knitting symbols into her shrouds--symbols which serve as a register of names for all those people who Defarge wants to pay when the revolutionaries rise. This revelation betrays Defarge's true nature as a vengeful and blood-thirsty radical. As the revolution gets underway, Madame Defarge's true nature is revealed for all to see. She turns much of her passion for vicious retribution on Lucie Manette, cultivating an obsessive vendetta against Lucie and her loved ones and escalating her vindictive behavior towards the family as the novel proceeds and the French Revolution takes on its full force.

Betraying his profound sympathies for the revolutionaries' plight, Dickens makes clear that Madame Defarge's ruthless viciousness does not stem from an inherent character defect, but rather from all she has suffered in her life. This suffering, as the reader learns later in the novel, was at the hands of the aristocracy, specifically the Evrémonde family, to which Charles Darnay is related by blood and Lucie Manette by marriage to Charles. Despite his sympathies however, Dickens stops short of showing support for Defarge's policy of retaliatory retribution against those who have harmed her and her family. In portraying Madame Defarge's death from her own gun's bullet, Dickens suggests that Defarge's passion for payback will eventually make her the oppressor of others, just as she was oppressed. Moreover, she digs her own grave by sewing seeds of such hate and discord in the revolution she helped to start.

Charles Darnay & Lucie Manette

Both Charles Darnay and Lucie Manette have the same underlying problem, which has perpetually bothered many readers since *A Tale of Two Cities* was written: they are both somewhat boring and one-dimensional, and neither of them grows or changes much over the course of the novel. Despite this seeming lack of depth, Darnay and Lucie both serve two important roles in the novel. First, their unyielding commitment to goodness, morality, and justice serves as a stark contrast to Madame Defarge's devotion to vengeful and retaliatory violence. Second, Darnay and Manette's continually manifested kindness and virtue inspires Sydney Carton to believe in a better future for himself and the possibility that he can become a better man.

Themes

Resurrection

Arising repeatedly throughout the novel, resurrection--both figuratively and literally--is one of the most important and overarching themes in *A Tale of Two Cities*. The first section of the novel is entitled "Recalled to Life," and is entirely focused on the rediscovery and rescue of Dr. Manette, who was thought to be dead but has actually imprisoned in the Bastille for eighteen years. The cryptic phrase "recalled to life" is the code for Mr. Lorry's and Lucie Manette's covert mission to Paris to rescue the Doctor. At one point, the phrase makes Mr. Lorry consider the ways in which being in prison as Doctor Manette was causes one to be disconnected from society for so long as that it is almost as if one has died. This theme also comes up again (in a more humorous way) in the handling of Jerry Cruncher's unsavory side-job as a "Resurrection-Man"--a profession that deals primarily with grave-robbing and selling body parts for profit. Interestingly, despite the unpleasant nature of Cruncher's occupation, it leads him to the discovery of Roger Cly's empty grave--showing that the spy never actually died as everyone had thought. By far the most notable reference to resurrection in the novel relates to the complex relationship between Charles Darnay and Sydney Carton. Early in the novel, Carton's likeness to Darnay saves the latter from conviction and execution during his trial in England. Then again, at the end of the novel, their resemblance allows Carton to take Darnay's place just before his execution at the hands of the French revolutionaries. These instances of resurrection are laden with religious overtones, connecting Carton's willingness to sacrifice his life for Darnay to Christ's sacrifice for humanity on the cross.

Fate & The Passage of Time

Throughout *A Tale of Two Cities*, Dickens frequently describes the passage of time and its connection to our fates as humans. Beginning in the very first chapter, with his references to trees awaiting their future as the guillotines of the French Revolution, Dickens suggests that this social movement was unavoidable. The novel's characters also individually sense the inevitability of Time and Fate. Lucie's interpretation of the noise she keeps hearing of feet echoing through the halls as suggesting that sometime in the future, the past would come back to haunt them; Darnay's sense that he must return to France, despite knowing the dangers there; Carton's sense that he must redeem himself by making significant sacrifices in the future--all of these continually draw upon the sense of inevitability associated with a Fate-driven universe. Throughout the novel, Fate is portrayed with a portentous tone rather than positive one. This dark tone is especially notable in Dickens's portrayal of Madame Defarge as resembling one of the Fates of classical tragic myth, which served to connect the future its ultimate dark ending.

Class Struggle

Unsurprisingly for a story that handles the French Revolution, class struggle is an overriding theme throughout the novel. Dickens clearly sympathizes with the motivations of the revolutionaries in France because of his own personal and political beliefs, which he demonstrates through his portrayal of the ruthlessness and cruelty of the aristocracy. Dickens clearly believes that there was significant justification for the peasants' desire for a societal overthrown. Ultimately however, despite his personal sympathies, Dickens sides with the argument against the Revolution, because of the overkill and bloodthirstiness of the revolutionaries as the movement gains more power. The novel also shows this transformation over the course of the story, demonstrating the evolution of the revolutionary movement from its focus on social justice and equality to a focus on retribution and revenge.

Inversions & Reversals

Related to the novel's focus on Class Struggle, this theme is also an inevitable result of astory surrounding a sociological event like the French Revolution. This Revolution completely mixed up French society and turned all of the societal norms on their heads. For example, upon his return to France, Darnay notes that in the new social order, noblemen are in prison with outlaws as their judges, juries, and executioners. This revolutionary society, however, allows for Carton to replace Darnay before the latter's execution--showing that in a system that has been turned so upside-down, a bad man can also take a good man's place.

Doubles & Duality

Another overarching aspect of the novel, Dickens introduces the theme of Doubles & Duality beginning with the very title of the novel, *A Tale of Two Cities*. Indeed, most of the characters and settings in the novel come in pairs--London/Paris and Darnay/ Carton, just to name a few examples--and are played off each other throughout the novel. Another important aspect of this theme is the oppositional nature of many of these pairs. For example, Madame Defarge's shadowy appearance and dark demeanor notably contrasts with Lucie Manette's light physicality and the bright morality of her character. This theme of contrasting doubles even arises in the language Dickens chooses to use throughout the story, especially notable in the novel's famous opening: "It was the best of times, it was the worst of times, it was the age of wisdom, it was the age of foolishness...".

Poverty & Social Injustice

Related to the theme of Class Struggle, Dickens places significant emphasis throughout the story on the poverty and social injustice that the French lower classes had been struggling against leading up to the Revolution. Because of his own radical progressive politics, Dickens maintained complicated feelings about the French Revolution--while he ultimately did not support the revolutionaries' barbarous tactics, he sympathized with their motives. As mentioned previously, Dickens writes in great depth and detail about the poverty and oppression the French peasants suffered and vividly illustrates the callous barbarity of the aristocracy, showing that he understands the lower classes' desire to overthrow the ruling order of French society. Moreover, because of Dickens's commitment to progressive politics, plot-lines related to this theme come up in many of Dickens's novels, especially *Hard Times* and *Oliver Twist*.

Family

Interestingly, considering the events happening in Dickens's personal life at the time he was writing, *A Tale of Two Cities* focuses heavily on the importance of commitment to family. Dickens introduces this theme early on, with Lucie Manette's trip to rescue her father in Paris, although she has not seen him for most of her life. This theme continues to feature prominently throughout the novel, as Lucie and Charles Darnay struggle to keep their family intact over the course of the story. Indeed, when Darnay faces a death sentence, his primary concern is for his family and their loss. And, as a final reinforcement of the family ideal, Carton sacrifices his own family-less life for Darnay's, therefore facilitating the preservation of the Darnay and Manette families.

Sacrifice

Related to the themes of Resurrection and Family, Dickens focuses on the necessity of sacrifice to achieve happiness in *A Tale of Two Cities*. Again, this theme arises both for characters personally, as well as on a more communal and national level throughout the novel. On a societal level, for example, the French revolutionaries demonstrate that the shift towards a more equitable France requires the sacrifice of many different individuals and groups in the country. On a more personal level, when Charles Darnay is arrested again in Chapter 7 of Book the Third, the guard tells Manette to remember that state and societal interests should trump personal needs and loyalties. Madame Defarge makes a similar point to her husband when she is criticizing his loyalty to Manette, which she believes undermines Defarge's willingness to sacrifice for the revolutionary cause. Finally, Carton's willingness to sacrifice his own life for Darnay's not only allows the Darnay-Manette family to stay intact, but also facilitates Carton's own moral rebirth.

Symbols

The Broken Wine Cask

Dickens uses this symbol, introduced early in the novel as a wine cask breaks outside the Defarge's wine-shop and peasants rush to collect the spilled wine, to show the bitter desperation of the French peasants leading up to the revolution. The hunger the lower classes experience is both literal and figurative--they are actually starving, but are also craving moral justice and political freedom in France. While this scene shows the peasants' intense hunger and poverty, it also foreshadows the violent bloodshed to come in the Revolution as the streets literally run red with wine (and, later, blood). Indeed, a drunken man actually uses the wine to scrawl "blood" on the wall, suggesting the barbarism to come.

Madame Defarge's Knitting

Madame Defarge uses actual symbols in her knitting to communicate with other members of the revolutionary movement (the symbols list names of those who would be condemned to death when the new revolutionary regime came to power). The knitting itself and the purpose behind it serves as a metaphor as well, however, of Madame Defarge's vengeful, malicious nature and, more broadly, the cunning and cold-blooded brutality of all the revolutionaries. Although Madame Defarge appears to be picture of calm, domestic femininity as she knits, she is actually sentencing her enemies to death. In a similar fashion, the impoverished and pitiable French peasants soon prove to be just as brutal and blindly violent as their former aristocratic oppressors. Significantly, Dickens's use of knitting imagery evokes the knitting and weaving traditionally associated with Fate in classical mythology, suggesting the inextricable link between vindictiveness and fate in the novel. Furthermore, Dickens's heavy reliance on this symbol suggests the timelessness of this tale throughout human history and the cyclical nature of fate and human destiny.

The Marquis

Although the Marquis de Evrémonde seems almost too ruthless and heartless to be believable as a true person, he is the ideal archetype of the brutality and corruption of the old social order in France. The Marquis's exploitation of and the disdain for the peasants in his area is especially obvious in his complete lack of empathy towards the father of the young boy his carriage tramples to death. The Marquis's behavior symbolizes the brutal aristocratic rule that the French peasants had had to endure for so long, and suggests Dickens's sympathy for the motivations of the revolutionaries.

Gold Thread

Lucie's golden blonde hair is emblematic of her magnetic beauty that attracts virtually every many she meets. Dickens uses her golden hair, however, to symbolize the goodness of her heart and how she binds her family together. He refers to her as "the golden thread" that keeps the family going. It is Lucie who connects Sydney Carton to Charles Darnay, Darnay to Doctor Manette, and Mr. Lorry to the family more broadly, and she is the motivation for many of the men in the story to pursue a greater purpose in their lives. Indeed, many of the characters give at least a passing thought to Lucie Manette's golden hair, suggesting that it has a symbolic power for many. For example, Jacques Three thinks about how much he'd like to see Lucie's golden hair on the guillotine's chopping block. Yet this will never come to pass, of course, as her hair also serves as something like a good luck charm for her and connects her to those she loves throughout the novel.

Imprisonment

More like a motif than an explicit symbol, the frequent occurrence of different forms of imprisonment in the novel serves as a symbol for the ways many of the different characters experience imprisonment in their own lives. Both Dr. Manette and Charles Darnay experience literal physical imprisonment in French fortresses. Yet, as the novel demonstrates, for many characters, including Manette and Madame Defarge, the memories of past bad experiences prove to be just as limiting and imprisoning as actually being in jail. Finally, for a character like Sydney Carton, his own choices in life have created a prison of his own making in which he feels his existence is meaningless--therefore, he is only able to break out of the "prison" of the life he has created, by sacrificing his own worthless life (in his eyes) for that of an admirable man like Darnay.

Climax

In Charles Darnay's second trial, Monsieur Defarge reads aloud a letter to the court that he has found, which was written by Dr. Manette during his imprisonment in the Bastille. In the letter--written many years before Dr. Manette ever knew Charles Darnay personally--Manette condemns Darnay as an heir of the heartless aristocratic Evrémonde family. In this climactic scene, the reader comes to understand that Madame Defarge will pursue Darnay with blood-thirsty zeal until the bitter end.

Structure

The novel is split into three books of varying lengths. Book One is relatively short with only six chapters, while both Books Two and Three are significantly longer, with 24 and 15 chapters respectively.

Teacher Guide - Relationship to Other Books

- Consider some of Dickens's other novels and writings. A full list of Dickens's other works can be found on <u>David Perdue's Charles Dickens Page.</u>
- Consider novels by Dickens's contemporaries and those who followed in his footsteps, such as Louisa May Alcott, Wilkie Collins, George Eliot, Henry James, and Mark Twain, among many others.
- Read some of the many critical essays and books available about *A Tale of Two Cities*. More information about some of the critical essays available can be found <u>here</u>.

Teacher Guide - Bringing in Technology

Day #1

- The Life and Times of Charles Dickens (ongoing activity): Students will use the internet to conduct research on Dickens's life and historical context.
- Timeline Game for Dickens's Life: Students will use the internet to conduct research about events in Dickens's life, and may use software or other computer-based tools to create timelines.

Day #2

- The Life and Times of Charles Dickens (ongoing activity): Students will use the internet to conduct research on Dickens's life and historical context.
- Evaluating Character in PBS Masterpiece's "A Tale of Two Cities": Depending on how the activity is constructed, a television, projector, or SmartBoard may be needed to watch the miniseries or clips from it.
- Poverty & Social Inequity in Late 18th and Early 19th Century England: Students will use the internet to conduct research on poverty and social inequity during Dickens's time.

Day #3

- The Life and Times of Charles Dickens (ongoing activity): Students will use the internet to conduct research on Dickens's life and historical context.
- Researching the Revolution: Students will use the internet to conduct research on the French Revolution.
- Acting out Scenes from "A Tale of Two Cities": Computers and access to document sharing software or web-based services will be useful for the writing and collaboration portions of this activity.

Day #4

- The Life and Times of Charles Dickens (ongoing activity): Students will use the internet to conduct research on Dickens's life and historical context.
- Creatively Representing the Characters from A Tale of Two Cities: Depending on the creative options available to students, computers may be useful for this activity.
- Surprise Scene Workshop, Part 1: Writing Your Own "A Tale of Two Cities" Scene: Computers and access to document sharing software or web-based services will be useful for the writing and collaboration portions of this activity.

Day #5

- The Life and Times of Charles Dickens (ongoing activity): Students will use the internet to conduct research on Dickens's life and historical context.

- Making a Movie: Adapting "A Tale of Two Cities" for Film: Computers, video cameras, video editing software, and any other desired devices could be used in this activity.
- Surprise Scene Workshop, Part 2: Creating Your Own Visualization of an "A Tale of Two Cities" Scene: Computers may be used, if desired, to give students the option to create audio-visual or graphic designs representations of students' poems.

Teacher Guide - Notes to the Teacher

The thought questions in this lesson plan provide material and ideas that students can use to write short original essays. For the sake of improving the power of expression, teachers should encourage students to write on topics that have been discussed in class, this time in the more formal writing style expected in a literary essay. At the same time, students should not be discouraged from choosing their own topics.

The questions provided for the final paper are most suitable for student essays. Remember that grading an essay should not depend on a simple checklist of required content.

Teacher Guide - Related Links

Charles Dickens Museum

http://dickensmuseum.com/

The website for 48 Doughty Street, the London home of Charles Dickens, which serves as the beautiful Charles Dickens Museum, has a wonderful array of information and resources about Charles Dickens.

The Victorian Web - Charles Dickens (1812-1870)

http://victorianweb.org/authors/dickens/index.html

This website has extensive resources available about Charles Dickens, as well as information about many other notable events and figures during the Victorian Age. A great resource for exploring Dickens's world more broadly.

History | The French Revolution

http://www.history.com/topics/french-revolution

This website is part of the History.com family of websites and provides numerous resources and research sources for students to learn more about the French Revolution and its impact domestically and abroad.

Teacher Guide - A Tale of Two Cities Bibliography

Eleanor Campisano, author of Lesson Plan. Completed on December 19, 2015, copyright held by GradeSaver.

Updated and revised by Michelle Rosenberg December 31, 2015. Copyright held by GradeSaver.

Dickens, Charles. A Tale of Two Cities. New York: Barnes & Noble Classics, 1859.

"Charles Dickens - Biography." Biography.com. 2015. 10/25/2015. <http://www.biography.com/people/charles-dickens-9274087>.

"BBC - History - Charles Dickens." BBC.co.uk. 2015. 10/25/2015. <http://www.bbc.co.uk/history/historic_figures/dickens_charles.shtml>.

"Masterpiece | The Tales of Charles Dickens - Dickens Resources | PBS." PBS.com. 2015. 10/31/2015. <http://www.pbs.org/wgbh/masterpiece/dickens/resources.html>.

"David Perdue's Charles Dickens Page - A Tale of Two Cities." David Perdue. 2015. 11/10/2015. <http://charlesdickenspage.com/cities.html>.

"A Tale of Two Cities: A Masterpiece Teacher's Guide." PBS.com. 2015. 12/1/2015. <http://d2buyft38glmwk.cloudfront.net/media/cms_page_media/10/Tale2Cities.pdf>.

Day 1 - Reading Assignment, Questions, Vocabulary

Students read the Preface to the First Edition and Book I.

Common Core Objectives

- CCSS.ELA-Literacy.CCRA.R.1 Read closely to determine what the text says explicitly and to make logical inferences from it; cite specific textual evidence when writing or speaking to support conclusions drawn from the text.

- CCSS.ELA-Literacy.CCRA.R.2 Determine central ideas or themes of a text and analyze their development; summarize the key supporting details and ideas.

- CCSS.ELA-Literacy.CCRA.R.4 Interpret words and phrases as they are used in a text, including determining technical, connotative, and figurative meanings, and analyze how specific word choices shape meaning or tone.

- CCSS.ELA-Literacy.CCRA.R.5 Analyze the structure of texts, including how specific sentences, paragraphs, and larger portions of the text (e.g., a section, chapter, scene, or stanza) relate to each other and the whole.

- CCSS.ELA-Literacy.CCRA.R.6 Assess how point of view or purpose shapes the content and style of a text.

- CCSS.ELA-Literacy.CCRA.R.10 Read and comprehend complex literary and informational texts independently and proficiently.

- CCSS.ELA-Literacy.CCRA.W.2 Write informative/explanatory texts to examine and convey complex ideas and information clearly and accurately through the effective selection, organization, and analysis of content.

- CCSS.ELA-Literacy.CCRA.W.7 Conduct short as well as more sustained research projects based on focused questions, demonstrating understanding of the subject under investigation.

Note that it is perfectly fine to expand any day's work into two days depending on the characteristics of the class, particularly if the class will engage in all of the suggested classroom exercises and activities and discuss all of the thought questions.

Content Summary for Teachers

Preface to the First Edition

Written in 1859 by the author himself, the Preface to the First Edition explains the other work that inspired Dickens to develop this story concept--*The Frozen Deep*, by Wilkie Collins. He then explains to the reader that, although inspired by Collins's work, *A Tale of Two Cities* is all his own. Finally, he assures the readers that, though some may doubt the accuracy of his portrayal of the "condition of the French people before or during the Revolution," it is based on reliable evidence.

Book I, Chapter 1

The novel begins in 1775 and is set in London and Paris, the capitals of two monarchical nations. Both countries are on the brink of revolution, and a growing sense of tumult and rebellion is spreading across both England and France. Highway robberies and thievery have become increasingly common, as have executions, even for minor infractions.

Book I, Chapter 2

A clerk at Tellson's Bank of London, Mr. Jarvis Lorry, is traveling to Dover via public mail-coach. Everyone in the coach is a stranger to each other and, due to the prevalence of highway robberies, all aboard, including the coachman, are wary. The coachman becomes afraid when he hears a horseman approach. The horserider, Jerry Cruncher, gives Mr. Lorry a message asking him to wait for a young woman in Dover, to which Mr. Lorry mysteriously replies, "recalled to life." After this strange exchange, Mr. Lorry continues on his journey to Dover, and Jerry considers his challenging journey from London and wonders about the strange response he received from Mr. Lorry.

Book I, Chapter 3

The chapter begins by discussing the ways in which all humans are mysteries to one another--although we may think we know who they are from the outside, we can never truly know what's going on beneath the surface. The three passengers bound for Dover all remain mysteries to each other. After meeting Mr. Lorry, Jerry returns to Temple Bar, still baffled by Mr. Lorry's cryptic reply to him.

As the coach continues to Dover, Mr. Lorry falls asleep and happily dreams of Tellson's Bank. A spirit then confronts Mr. Lorry--a man who has been buried for eighteen years and has clawed his way out. Mr. Lorry has a dream conversation with the spirit, repeatedly confirming that he has been buried for eighteen years. The sunrise awakens Mr. Lorry and, as he watches the countryside pass by, he pities the man who would be buried away from nature for such a long time.

Book I, Chapter 4

Mr. Lorry arrives in Dover and settles into his hotel with breakfast on his own. He speaks with a waiter, telling him that Tellson's Bank has branches in both London and Paris, but Mr. Lorry himself has not traveled to Paris for fifteen years. After a peaceful few hours alone, Mr. Lorry is interrupted by a woman referred to as Mam'selle (Miss Manette) insisting that she must see him immediately.

Upon seeing her, Mr. Lorry becomes emotional as he remembers carrying her across the Channel as a baby. An orphan whose finances are managed by Tellson's Bank, Miss Manette was told that Mr. Lorry would be accompanying her as she traveled to France and that he would also have a surprising message for her. Mr. Lorry struggles to compose himself, but is finally able to explain to Miss Manette that her French father was actually still alive in France. He had been imprisoned for many years, but was now free and living in Paris.

Miss Manette is worried about going to see her father, knowing he must be recovering from a very difficult period. Mr. Lorry explains that their mission is actually to bring her father back to England with them--but that they should avoid talking about it overtly, instead referring to the experience as being "recalled to life." Miss Manette is overwhelmed and faints, and her servant comes to her rescue with smelling-salts.

Book I, Chapter 5

In Paris, a cask of wine outside of Monsieur Defarge's wine-shop falls and breaks, spilling wine all over the street. Everyone stops and drinks wine off the street, all clearly marked by desperate hunger. The street signs reflect the general mood of the people--the baker's sign is painted with only tiny loaves of bread and the bucher's sign is shows just meat scraps. Only the people's weaponry seems to have the appearance of vigor and might.

Monsieur Defarge discusses the wine incident with Gaspard, who writes "blood" on the wall in a mixture of wine and mud. Defarge returns to his shop and his wife gestures that he should see who's there. Mr. Lorry and Miss Manette are waiting for Defarge, along with three men all named Jacques. After Defarge takes the three men to a room they wish to see, Mr. Lorry and Miss Manette reveal their identities and ask to see Dr. Manette.

Mr. Lorry is annoyed both that Dr. Manette is locked in the apartment and that they can see the three Jacques spying on them through cracks in the walls. Miss Manette is afraid but enters anyway and finds her father making shoes.

Book I, Chapter 6

Initially, Dr. Manette barely notices his visitors and, when asked his name, responds, "One Hundred and Five, North Tower." He says he learned how to make shoes "here" (i.e. in prison), because he thinks he's still imprisoned.

Dr. Manette seems to vaguely recognize Mr. Lorry, but he is taken aback at seeing his daughter. He recognizes her golden curls, and they weep together over the wrongs they've both endured.

Miss Manette requests her father be moved from Paris and preparations are made. As he comes out of the garret, he's confused that he's not coming out of the prison where he thought he was. Book I concludes with Mr. Lorry considering how to restore a resurrected man.

Thought Questions (students consider while they read)

1. Why do you think that Dickens wrote the Preface to the First Edition? What does it contribute to the novel and the reader's understanding of Dickens's purpose in writing it?

2. How does Dickens set the ominous, foreboding tone of *A Tale of Two Cities* from the very beginning of the novel?

3. At this point in your reading, what do you think the significance of the title and the opening paragraph of the novel might be?

4. What is the significance of the scene in which the wine cask breaks outside the Defarge's wine-shop?

5. What is the underlying meaning of the phrase "recalled to life"? How do Mr. Lorry's reflections on Manette's release from prison relate to larger themes related to resurrection?

Vocabulary (in order of appearance)

"...that magnificent potentate the Lord Mayor of London..." (I.1)

potentate:

A leader or ruler, especially one who is totalitarian.

"...and the majesty of the law fired blunderbusses in among them, loaded with rounds of shot and ball..." (I.1)

blunderbuss:

An old-fashioned rifle-like firearm.

"...and to-morrow of a wretched pilferer who had robbed a farmer's boy of sixpence." (I.1)

pilferer:

Petty thief.

"...where a loaded blunderbuss lay at the top of six or eight loaded horse-pistols, deposited on a substratum of cutlass." (I.2)

substratum:

A lower or underlying layer of something, usually soil or rock.

cutlass:

A short sword with a slightly curved blade, similar to a machete.

"If any one of the three had hd the hardihood to propose to another to walk on a little ahead into the mist and darkness..." (I.2)

hardihood:

Daring, bravery.

"With this hurried adjuration, he cocked his blunderbuss, and stood on the offensive." (I.2)

adjuration:

A sincere request, solemn entreaty.

"...who had expeditiously secreted their watches and purses in their boots..." (I.2)

expeditiously:

Speedily, promptly.

"...it is inexorable consolidation and perpetuation of the secret that was always in that individuality..." (I.3)

inexorable:

Unstoppable, inevitable.

"...and a loud watch ticking a sonorous sermon under his flapped waist-coat..." (I.4)

sonorous:

Resonant, full of sound.

"The gentleman from Tellson's had nothing left for it but to empty his glass with an air of stolid desperation..." (I.4)

stolid:

Unemotional, stoic.

"The likeness passed away, say, like a breath along the surface of the gaunt pier-glass behind her..." (I.4)

gaunt:

Lean, spindly, haggard.

"'I pass my whole life, miss, in turning an immense pecuniary Mangle.'" (I.4)

pecuniary:

Related to finances or money.

"...bringing his left hand from the back of the chair to lay it on the supplicatory fingers that clasped him..." (I.4)

supplicatory:

Humble, prayerful (of an action or gesture).

"...fluttered in every vestige of a gsrment tht the wind shook." (I.5)

vestige:

Remnant, trace.

"Hunger was shred into atomies in every farthing porringer of husky chips of potato..." (I.5)

farthing:

An old monetary unit from England, approximately equal to a quarter of a penny.

porringer:

A shallow dish, often used for serving porridge

"With an admonitory gesture to keep them back..." (I.5)

admonitory:

Conveying a warning or correction.

"This time, a pair of haggard eyes had looked at the questioner, before the face had dropped again." (I.6)

haggard:

Looking exhausted or unwell, gaunt.

"...there was nothing else in the garret but a pallet bed..." (I.6)

garret:

An attic room, especially one that is small and dank.

Additional Homework

1. Complete some preliminary research on Charles Dickens's life and write a brief (1-2 page) biographical summary of Dickens's life.

2. Following up on Day #1's classroom activity on Dickensian Descriptions, think about a place, area, or neighborhood you're very familiar with and consider how you would describe it. Then, write a 1-2 page description of the place, mimicking Dickens's style.

Day 1 - Discussion of Thought Questions

1. Why do you think that Dickens wrote the Preface to the First Edition? What does it contribute to the novel and the reader's understanding of Dickens's purpose in writing it?

Time:

5-7 minutes

Discussion:

The Preface to the First Edition of the novel was written in 1859 by Dickens himself. In this Preface, Dickens explains the other work that inspired him to develop this story concept--*The Frozen Deep*, by Wilkie Collins. He then explains to the reader that, although inspired by Collins's work, *A Tale of Two Cities* is all his own. Finally, he assures the readers that, though some may doubt the accuracy of his portrayal of the "condition of the French people before or during the Revolution," it is based on reliable evidence.

These final lines of the Preface are particularly notable, especially as the shocking events leading up to the French Revolution and the gruesome realities of the Revolution itself unfold over the course of the novel. Dickens wants to make the point early on that, although some of the peasants' conditions may seem so awful as to be unbelievable and events that took place may seem implausibly horrific, everything he wrote was based in fact. Dickens wants to make sure that readers know that, while this is a novel and not a true historical text, it is a relatively accurate portrayal of both sides of the arguments for and against the French Revolution.

2. How does Dickens set the ominous, foreboding tone of *A Tale of Two Cities* from the very beginning of the novel?

Time:

7-10 minutes

Discussion:

As a reminder, after a short, scene-setting first chapter, the second chapter of the novel finds Mr. Lorry traveling to Dover via public mail-coach. Everyone in the coach is a stranger to each other and, due to the prevalence of highway robberies, all aboard, including the coachman, are wary. The coachman becomes afraid when he hears a horseman approach. The horserider, Jerry Cruncher, gives Mr. Lorry a message asking him to wait for a young woman in Dover, to which Mr. Lorry mysteriously replies, "recalled to life." After this strange exchange, Mr. Lorry continues on his journey to Dover, and Jerry considers his challenging journey from London and wonders about the strange response he received from Mr. Lorry.

This first scene where the reader meets some of the novel's main characters is full of dark and creepy details, such as the mist-covered road to Dover, the wariness of the coach's passengers, and Jerry Cruncher's sudden and mysterious appearance out of nowhere. These gloomy and mysterious opening scenes serve the simultaneous purposes of giving the novel a ominous gothic atmosphere and foreshadowing some of the dark events to come in subsequent chapters as the true force of the French Revolution makes itself known. Furthermore, this initial scene-setting, filled with mysterious shadows and cryptic secrets, reveals what will become a continual theme throughout the novel: that all humans are mysteries to each other, and Fate plays an enigmatic role in all of our lives.

3. At this point in your reading, what do you think the significance of the title and the opening paragraph of the novel might be?

Time:

7-10 minutes

Discussion:

The opening paragraph of *A Tale of Two Cities*--"It was the best of times, it was the worst of times, it was the age of wisdom, it was the age of foolishness, it was the epoch of belief, it was the epoch of incredulity, it was the season of Light, it was the season of Darkness, it was the spring of hope, it was the winter of despair, we had everything before us, we had nothing before us, we were all going direct to Heaven, we were all going direct the other way--in short, the period was so far like the present period, that some of its noisiest authorities insisted on its being received, for good or for evil, in the superlative degree of comparison only"--is one of the most famous sets of opening lines in all of Western literature. Furthermore, these opening lines, along with the title drive home the importance early on of the theme of Doubles & Duality in the novel.

At this point in students' reading, they may not have gotten to the point of discussing all of the relevant novel's themes that this opening passage reflects, so some of these discussion points many not yet be completely relevant. However, discussing these lines may provide a good introduction to several important themes of the story. For example, these lines clearly reveal Dickens's own perspectives on the political and sociological changes happening leading up to the Revolution and during his own era. In addition, these lines relate to the cyclical sense of the past echoing into the future that Dickens hearkens back to so often over the course of the novel. In particular, in addition to its clear focus on the recurrent theme of Doubles & Duality, this opening paragraph also foreshadows the importance of two other themes in the novel: Class Struggle and Inversions & Reversals.

4. What is the significance of the scene in which the wine cask breaks outside the Defarge's wine-shop?

Time:

7-10 minutes

Discussion:

Dickens uses the symbol of the broken wine cask--introduced in this scene early in the novel as a wine cask breaks outside the Defarge's wine-shop and peasants rush to collect the spilled wine--to show the bitter desperation of the French peasants leading up to the revolution. The hunger the lower classes experience is both literal and figurative--they are actually starving, but are also craving moral justice and political freedom in France.

While this scene shows the peasants' intense hunger and poverty, it also foreshadows the violent bloodshed to come in the Revolution as the streets literally run red with wine (and, later, blood). Indeed, a drunken man actually uses the wine to scrawl "blood" on the wall, suggesting the barbarism to come.

5. What is the underlying meaning of the phrase "recalled to life"? How do Mr. Lorry's reflections on Manette's release from prison relate to larger themes related to resurrection?

Time:

5-7 minutes

Discussion:

The first section of the novel is entitled "Recalled to Life," and is entirely focused on the rediscovery and rescue of Dr. Manette, who was thought to be dead but has actually imprisoned in the Bastille for eighteen years. The cryptic phrase "recalled to life" is the code for Mr. Lorry's and Lucie Manette's covert mission to Paris to rescue the Doctor. At one point, the phrase makes Mr. Lorry consider the ways in which being in prison as Doctor Manette was causes one to be disconnected from society for so long as that it is almost as if one has died.

The phrase "recalled to life" serves two primary purposes in this first section of the story, as well as the novel overall. First, the phrase adds to the mysterious and ominous gothic tone of the novel by cryptically communicating to Mr. Lorry and Lucie Manette that Dr. Manette will imminently be released from prison. Second, these words foreshadow the theme of resurrection, which comes up literally and symbolically repeatedly throughout the novel.

Day 1 - Short Answer Evaluation

1. In what year was A Tale of Two Cities written?

   _____

2. In what play does Charles Dickens say he was acting in with his children and friends when he came up with the main idea for "A Tale of Two Cities"?

   _____

3. What is the name of the bank at which Mr. Lorry works?

   _____

4. Where is Mr. Lorry traveling to via coach at the beginning of the novel?

   _____

5. Who comes to bring Mr. Lorry a letter?

   _____

6. What is Mr. Lorry's cryptic reply to the message that is brought him during his journey?

   _____

7. Where was Miss Manette's father imprisoned?

   _____

8. Who accompanies Lucie Manette to Paris to rescue her father?

   _____

9. What does Gaspard write on the wall outside the Defarge's wine shop?

_____

10. Who spies on Dr. Manette in the apartment he's locked up in?

_____

Answer Key

1. 1859.
2. Wilkie Collins's "The Frozen Deep."
3. Tellson's Bank of London.
4. Dover.
5. Jerry Cruncher.
6. Mr. Lorry responds "recalled to life."
7. Paris.
8. Mr. Lorry.
9. Blood.
10. The three Jacques.

Day 1 - Crossword Puzzle

ACROSS

4. Leader or ruler, often totalitarian.
7. _____ brings Mr. Lorry a letter during his journey.
9. Unemotional, stoic.
10. A short sword, like a machete.
13. Lean, spindly, haggard.
14. At the beginning, _____ is imprisoned in Paris.
17. Dr. Manette likes to make _____.
18. At 12, Dickens went to work in a _____ factory.
19. A sincere request.
20. Petty thief.

DOWN

1. Dickens's father was imprisoned for _____
2. The two primary cities in the novel are London and _____
3. The Defarges run a _____ shop.
5. Speedily, promptly.
6. Remnant, trace.
8. The three _____ are followers of the Defarges.
11. Resonant, full of sound.
12. Unstoppable, inevitable
15. Mr. Lorry works at _____'s Bank
16. Daring, bravery.

Crossword Puzzle Answer Key

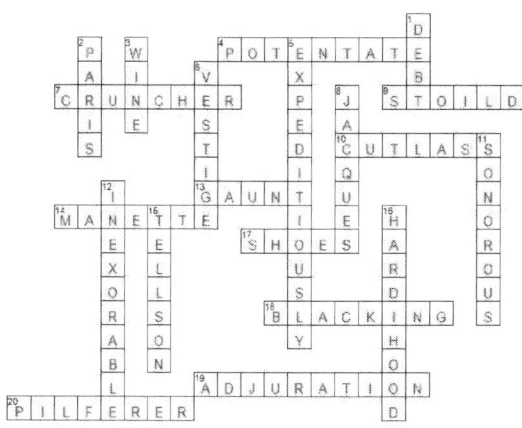

ACROSS

4. Leader or ruler; often totalitarian.
7. _____ brings Mr. Lorry a letter during his journey.
9. Unemotional, stoic.
10. A short sword, like a machete.
13. Lean, spindly, haggard.
14. At the beginning, _____ is imprisoned in Paris.
17. Dr. Manette likes to make _____.
18. At 12, Dickens went to work in a _____ factory.
19. A sincere request.
20. Petty thief.

DOWN

1. Dickens's father was imprisoned for _____.
2. The two primary cities in the novel are London and _____.
3. The Defarges run a _____ shop.
5. Speedily, promptly.
6. Remnant, trace.
8. The three _____ are followers of the Defarges.
11. Resonant, full of sound.
12. Unstoppable, inevitable.
15. Mr. Lorry works at _____'s Bank.
16. Daring, bravery.

Day 1 - Vocabulary Quiz

Terms

1. _____ blunderbuss
2. _____ hardihood
3. _____ adjuration
4. _____ expeditiously
5. _____ inexorable
6. _____ sonorous
7. _____ stolid
8. _____ gaunt
9. _____ supplicatory
10. _____ admonitory

Answers

A. A sincere request, solemn entreaty.
B. Speedily, promptly.
C. Humble, prayerful (of an action or gesture).
D. Daring, bravery.
E. Conveying a warning or correction.
F. Unstoppable, inevitable.
G. Lean, spindly, haggard.
H. An old-fashioned rifle-like firearm.
I. Resonant, full of sound.
J. Unemotional, stoic.

Answer Key

1. H blunderbuss: An old-fashioned rifle-like firearm.
2. D hardihood: Daring, bravery.
3. A adjuration: A sincere request, solemn entreaty.
4. B expeditiously: Speedily, promptly.
5. F inexorable: Unstoppable, inevitable.
6. I sonorous: Resonant, full of sound.
7. J stolid: Unemotional, stoic.
8. G gaunt: Lean, spindly, haggard.
9. C supplicatory: Humble, prayerful (of an action or gesture).
10. E admonitory: Conveying a warning or correction.

Day 1 - Classroom Activities

1. The Life and Times of Charles Dickens

Kind of Activity:

Long-term Project

Objective:

Students will be able to conduct research on life in late 18th and early 19th century England, examine how specific societal changes may have impacted Dickens's life and writings, and present their research and findings to the class.

Common Core Standards:

CCSS.ELA-Literacy.CCRA.R.4, CCSS.ELA-Literacy.CCRA.R.5

Time:

20-25 minutes (recurring)

Structure:

In order to understand Dickens's *A Tale of Two Cities*, it is important for students to understand the context in which Dickens wrote, and the ways in which Dickens's world impacted his beliefs and writing style. This recurring group activity will include multiple parts:
*Small group research on topics relating to Dickens's life and times
*Connecting the assigned research topic to the day's readings, and
*Presenting their research to the class in a comprehensive way that covers the full breadth of the assigned topic and the relevant scenes.

For Day #1, introduce the activity and walk the class through the world events and societal developments in England happening during Dickens's lifetime that could have impacted his perspectives about particular important themes in his writing. For example, identify the French Revolution and the rule of Queen Victoria as a significant cultural shift in England that impacted Dickens's and others' worldviews. Then identify a textual example of this theme arising in his writing. Next, check for understanding, asking students questions about the observations and inferences made about the selected theme. Then, depending on student understanding, lead students in a guided practice--identifying another event or aspect of Dickens's life and a textual example of a related theme--or proceed to splitting students into groups.

Have each group select (or assign each group) their assigned theme for the remainder of this project. Themes might include: Science & Technology; Rebellions/ Revolutions in the late 18th and early 19th centuries; Queen Victoria's reign; Dickens's Religious Worldview/Outlook, Dickens's Literary & Philosophical influences; Literature in the Victorian era, Cultural/Religious Reactions to the French Revolution, etc.

Provide biographical sources on Dickens for students to read independently, or have them begin conducting their own research, depending on the time and resources available. These resources could include any of the following, in addition to many others:

Victorian England:

- http://www.english.uwosh.edu/roth/VictorianEngland.htm
- http://www.bbc.co.uk/history/british/victorians/
- http://www.aboutbritain.com/articles/victorian-era-1837-1901.asp
- https://www.wwnorton.com/college/english/nael/victorian/review/ summary.htm
- http://www.history.ac.uk/ihr/Focus/Victorians/article.html
- https://www.history.org.uk/resources/primary_resource_3871_134.html

Charles Dickens:

- http://www.biography.com/people/charles-dickens-9274087
- http://www.bbc.co.uk/history/historic_figures/dickens_charles.shtml
- http://www.online-literature.com/dickens/
- http://www.britannica.com/biography/Charles-Dickens-British-novelist
- http://www.dickens-online.info/charles-dickens-biography.htm
- http://www.pbs.org/wgbh/masterpiece/dickens/dickens.html
- http://charlesdickenspage.com/
- http://dickensmuseum.com/
- http://dickenslive.com/
- http://www.dickensfellowship.org/life-charles-dickens

A Tale of Two Cities Analysis:

- http://www.gradesaver.com/tale-of-two-cities
- http://www.novelguide.com/a-tale-of-two-cities/theme-analysis
- http://www.litcharts.com/lit/a-tale-of-two-cities/plot-overview
- http://www.online-literature.com/dickens/twocities/
- http://charlesdickenspage.com/cities.html
- http://www.pbs.org/wgbh/masterpiece/archive/110/110.html

Each small group will then discuss important events related to their group's assigned theme, while the scribe begins to chart the events that could have shaped Dickens's perspectives on that theme. Next, each group will examine the day's readings to find textual examples of the theme. The group will then analyze their selected pieces of textual evidence and add them to their overall analysis.

Students will then share out one preliminary finding from their group with the whole class.

Ideas for Differentiated Instruction:

- Provide texts at a variety of reading levels depending on student ability.
- Provide some groups with the option to read aloud the biographical section, or listen to/watch audio or video pieces about Dickens as a form of research.
- Assign students different roles—scribe, head researcher, lead note-taker, presenter, etc.—based on skills or areas for growth.
- Split students into groups by skill-set or areas of need, so that some groups can work more independently, and the teacher can support other groups as needed.

Assessment Ideas:

- Student groups each generate a series of charts about an aspect of life or culture in Dickens's time and how it related to his writings, with specific references to scenes from *A Tale of Two Cities*.
- Students present findings from group charts to the rest of the class.
- Students take notes in interactive handouts on other groups' theme presentations.

2. Timeline Game for Dickens's Life

Kind of Activity:

Group Work

Objective:

Students will be able to conduct brief research about events in Dickens's life and consider how they may have impacted his writing.

Common Core Standards:

CCSS.ELA-Literacy.CCRA.R.6, CCSS.ELA-Literacy.CCRA.R.10

Time:

25-30 minutes

Structure:

Scholars and literary critics have long believed that Dickens's writing was strongly influenced by experiences and events in his life that impacted his worldview and beliefs. In this introductory activity, students will order different events in Dickens's life, first in small groups, then together as a class. Then students will conduct brief research on a specific event or experience in Dickens's life, and write about it (individually or as a group), arguing for how it uniquely impacted Dickens's writing.

Prior to class, select 30 to 40 important events from Dickens's life (e.g. Dickens was born, Dickens goes to work in the blacking factory after his father goes to debtor's prison, Dickens clerks for an attorney, etc.) and write them out in order on post-it notes. These key events/experiences can be selected from the Biography of Charles Dickens, and supplemented with any of the following resources on Charles Dickens's life and times:

- Timeline of important events in Charles Dickens's life
- The Biography.com Webpage about Charles Dickens
- The BBC.com Webpage about Charles Dickens
- The Encyclopedia of World Biography's piece on Charles Dickens
- An Additional Biography of Charles Dickens and his world
- The Dickens Project--a good source for additional research and information about Dickens

Next, separate the individual events/experiences into random groups of 8-10. Place these groups of slips of paper into envelopes for each group (one envelope per group). In addition, create a large timeline, either on the board or on chart paper, which will fit the full scope of Dickens's life, and allow for students to put the post-it notes/pieces of paper in the appropriate year/date on the timeline. Finally, create an interactive handout, in which students can put all of the events listed on the big timeline into their own individual version, and which they can hand in for assessment after the second part of the activity (the writing activity) is completed as well. Alternatively, use a digital timeline tool like www.dipity.com to streamline the process, perhaps with students each creating their own timeline on a tablet and then working as a class on a larger computer or SMART board.

Split students into small groups (4-5 students each) and distribute the envelopes and interactive handouts. Have students work as a group to determine the date/timeframe and order of the events in their envelope, then have students come to the large timeline (on the board/chart paper) to place their events at the appropriate point on the timeline.

Next, each group will conduct more in-depth research on one of Dickens's life events. After they have completed their small group research, students will independently write 2-3 paragraphs about the importance of this event/experience in Dickens's life and writing.

Ideas for Differentiated Instruction:

- Assign students different roles—scribe, head researcher, lead note-taker, presenter, etc.—based on skills or areas for growth.
- Give different groups or students different events/experiences to research and write about, depending on their analysis and research skill level.
- Provide some groups with the option to read aloud the biographical section, or listen to/watch audio or video pieces about Dickens as a form of research.
- Split students into groups by skill-set or areas of need, so that some groups can work more independently, and the teacher can support other groups more.

Assessment Ideas:

- Each student completes a timeline, as well as an individual writing assignment on the importance of their assigned event/experience for research.
- Student groups each generate a chart about their assigned area for further research from Dickens's life events/experiences.
- Students present findings from group charts to the rest of the class.

3. Dickensian Descriptions

Kind of Activity:

Group Discussion

Objective:

Students will closely examine a few selected scens from "A Tale of Two Cities," evaluate and discuss the images Dickens presents as they imagine them based on the descriptions, and present their discussion points and observations to the class.

Common Core Standards:

CCSS.ELA-Literacy.CCRA.R.2, CCSS.ELA-Literacy.CCRA.R.4, CCSS.ELA-Literacy.CCRA.W.3, CCSS.ELA-Literacy.CCRA.SL.2

Time:

30-35 minutes

Structure:

This activity helps students to look closely at Dickens's imagery, evaluate his in-depth descriptions of people and surroundings, and discuss how he creates the evocative scenes and descriptions of events that he is so well known for.

In small groups, have students find three descriptions from the readings thus far that are particularly good examples of the Dickensian descriptive style.

Distribute a worksheet or digital collaborative document with the following set of steps for students to complete (individually or in small groups):

- Find three examples of Dickensian descriptions and imagery in the novel, and write their location below.
- Beneath each example, briefly explain or summarize the imagery used and its significance.
- Choose one example and write or type it out in its entirety.
- Annotate the full example.
- Underline words that are unfamiliar, tricky, or that have multiple layers of meaning.
- Italicize words or phrases that are particularly evocative or significant.
- Write down and evaluate 2-3 literary devices that Dickens uses to create his evocative imagery.

Next, have each small student group choose one short passage to evaluate and examine the imagery. Have students use dictionaries to look up words in the quotations. Looking up words can introduce students to new words with which they were previously unfamiliar, and can also introduce students to secondary definitions of the words. In addition, have students underline or highlight specific words and/or phrases that they find evocative. You may wish to demonstrate good practices for annotation on an overhead projector or interactive whiteboard.

Finally, have student groups present 3-5 of their group's annotations, scene evaluation elements, and take-aways from their discussions to the full class.

Ideas for Differentiated Instruction:

- Give students different media as options for ways to present their ideas, to allow for students with different learning styles to best express what they've learned.
- For the discussion section or if doing group work, use mixed-level groupings, allowing students to play to their different strengths.
- You may wish to provide the examples of imagery, rather than having students find their own.

Assessment Ideas:

- Students can fill out individual interactive handouts during the discussion section of the activity, in order to demonstrate their personal understanding of the material.
- The interactive handout can be graded for expression of ideas, support of thesis, and mechanics.
- The group presentation can be graded for completion, participation, acuity of observations, and the thoroughness of its analysis of the scene/chapter section.

Day 2 - Reading Assignment, Questions, Vocabulary

Students read Book II, Chapters 1-10.

Common Core Objectives

- CCSS.ELA-Literacy.CCRA.R.5 Analyze the structure of texts, including how specific sentences, paragraphs, and larger portions of the text (e.g., a section, chapter, scene, or stanza) relate to each other and the whole.

- CCSS.ELA-Literacy.CCRA.R.7 Integrate and evaluate content presented in diverse media and formats, including visually and quantitatively, as well as in words.

- CCSS.ELA-Literacy.CCRA.W.2 Write informative/explanatory texts to examine and convey complex ideas and information clearly and accurately through the effective selection, organization, and analysis of content.

- CCSS.ELA-Literacy.CCRA.W.7 Conduct short as well as more sustained research projects based on focused questions, demonstrating understanding of the subject under investigation.

- CCSS.ELA-Literacy.CCRA.W.8 Gather relevant information from multiple print and digital sources, assess the credibility and accuracy of each source, and integrate the information while avoiding plagiarism.

- CCSS.ELA-Literacy.CCRA.SL.6 Adapt speech to a variety of contexts and communicative tasks, demonstrating command of formal English when indicated or appropriate.

- CCSS.ELA-Literacy.CCRA.R.3 Analyze how and why individuals, events, or ideas develop and interact over the course of a text.

- CCSS.ELA-Literacy.CCRA.R.2 Determine central ideas or themes of a text and analyze their development; summarize the key supporting details and ideas.

Note that it is perfectly fine to expand any day's work into two days depending on the characteristics of the class, particularly if the class will engage in all of the suggested classroom exercises and activities and discuss all of the thought questions.

Content Summary for Teachers

Book II, Chapter 1

Book II begins by describing Tellson's Bank. Those who work there love the bank's dark and deteriorating interior and believe it should remain inconvenient and uncomfortable because that is the way it has always been.

Jerry Cruncher works for Tellson's, doing whatever odd jobs they need him to do. He lives with his devoted wife in a tiny apartment in Whitefriars, whom he regularly abuses for praying. He worries that Mrs. Cruncher will pray against him, so gets his son to keep watch over her and tell him about any secret praying.

Jerry Cruncher's son comes with him to work, and often wonders where the rust comes from on the straw Cruncher gnaws on. Though there is presumably no rust involved in his job at Tellson's, Cruncher always has rust on him.

Book II, Chapter 2

A clerk at Tellson's gives Jerry Cruncher a message for Mr. Lorry, who is attending Charles Darnay's trial at Old Bailey. Jerry makes his way to the trial. Another onlooker assures him that this is the trial of Charles Darnay for treason, and tells Jerry of the quartering that will be the likely punishment resulting from this trial. Charles Darnay enters. He pled not guilty the day before and, as he enters the courtroom, he sees Dr. and Miss Manette, both of whom are supposed to be prosecution witnesses.

Book II, Chapter 3

Charles Darnay is charged with treason for being a spy for France against England, allegedly as far back as five years ago, during the beginning of the American Revolution. John Barsad, a former friend, serves as as the primary witness against him. Mr. Lorry, Miss Manette, and Dr. Manette also testify against Charles Darnay.

The trial is thrown into disarray when Mr. Carton--a man who looks almost identical to Darnay--reveals himself. In addition, Darnay's defense lawyer, Mr. Stryver, demonstrates that Barsad also committed traitorous acts, undermining his credibility. As the jury deliberates at length, Miss Manette (Lucie) swoons and must be removed from the courthouse. Mr. Lorry asks Jerry to wait to receive the verdict to take back to Tellson's and, shortly thereafter, Jerry learns that Darnay is acquitted.

Book II, Chapter 4

Dr. Manette, Lucie, Mr. Lorry, the defense solicitor, Mr. Stryver all congratulate Darnay on his acquittal. Dr. Manette is feeling troubled by the cross-examination he endured about his imprisonment. The Manettes leave, while Mr. Carton and Mr. Darnay go to a tavern to talk. Mr. Carton proposes a toast to Miss Manette. After Darnay departs, Carton reflects on his resentment of Darnay--he is too much like what Carton could've become had he not been such a degenerate. He also resents Darnay for making Miss Manette look on Carton with pity and kindness.

Book II, Chapter 5

Mr. Stryver and Mr. Carton are drinking partners and former classmates. Although he was already ambitious, Mr. Stryver became a much more successful lawyer when Mr. Carton began to work as his assistant. Stryver mentions Miss Manette's attractiveness, but Carton says that she is just a blonde "doll." Carton returns home and weeps over his lost potential.

Book II, Chapter 6

Four months after the end of Darnay's trial, Mr. Lorry is having dinner with the Manettes at their home in Soho. At this point, Dr. Manette has restarted his medical practice. Before the Manette's arrive, Miss Pross is complaining to Mr. Lorry about the "hundreds of people" who come looking for her "Ladybird," Miss Manette. Miss Pross does not think any of them are deserving of Lucie. Mr. Lorry admires Miss Pross's devotion to the Manettes, and asks her whether Dr. Manette knows who caused his lengthy imprisonment, to which she replies that she thinks she does know. Shortly thereafter, Lucie and Dr. Manette arrive, and Miss Pross fusses over Lucie's appearance. Miss Pross then cooks dinner for the group, having learned many cooking tricks from French expatriates in the area.

After their dinner, Mr. Darnay arrives. Dr. Manette begins the evening in good spirits, but his mood darkens when Darnay tells a story about the Tower of London. Darnay talks about the initials of former prisoners carved in the walls and one set of initials--D.I.G.--that could not be matched to anyone.

Later, Mr. Carton joins the group. Lucie talks about her thinking of the footsteps she hears outside her house as those of people coming in and out of her life; Mr. Carton responds that this daydream may actually represent of the many people who are or will be part of her life.

Book II, Chapter 7

Monseigneur is a powerful French lord who leads a privileged life, divorced from the realities most of his subjects have to endure on a daily basis. He holds receptions biweekly in a Paris hotel and requires four servants to ceremoniously serve him his morning chocolate. He tends to let general business run its own course, unless it directly impacts him, in which case he tries to make the outcome as beneficial to him as possible. He has allied himself with a Farmer-General through marrying his sister off to one of them. Virtually everyone in Monseigneur's court has no idea how do anything that is useful to the greater public. This lack of social responsibility and understanding leads Marquis de Evrémonde (also called Monseigneur) to condemn the first Monseigneur before leaving his court.

Driving recklessly, Monseigneur's carriage kills a child in the road. The Marquis gives a gold coin to Gaspard, the child's father, and another gold coin to Defarge as a reward for observing that the child is probably luckier to be dead. As the Marquis drives off, Defarge hurls the coin after the carriage. The rich continue to recklessly drive their carriages through Saint Antoine as the many hungry and impoverished observe from the sides of the road.

Book II, Chapter 8

Driving through another impoverished village--one made poor through excessive taxation--the Marquis stops to berate one of the villagers over staring at him as he drove up the hill. The villager responds that there was a ghostly white, very tall man hanging on under the carriage as it drove up the hill; when the carriage stopped, the man disappeared over the hillside. Annoyed, the Marquis asks the Postmaster, Monsieur Gabelle, to banish all the villagers from his sight. After setting off again, the Marquis is again stopped by woman with a petition. She wants to mark her recently-dead husband's grave with a piece of wood or stone; in fact, many others have died recently and just be heaped into the earth, as most villagers have no money to pay for any sort of marker for the dead. The Marquis pushes her out of the way, ignoring her request, and continues on towards his château. Upon his arrival, he asks if Monsieur Charles (i.e. Charles Darnay) had arrived from England.

Book II, Chapter 9

Monseigneur's château is entirely made of stone, as if a Gorgon's head (e.g. Medusa) had looked on it. Complaining that his nephew hasn't arrived, Monseigneur has his dinner. Upon Darnay's arrival, Monseigneur notes that it has taken him a long time to make his way from London. Darnay says that the Monseigneur used a letter de cachet to try to have him imprisoned, which Monseigneur doesn't deny. Rather, Monseigneur complains that these measures are increasingly inaccessible as the French aristocracy has lost many of its former powers. He argues that repression of the masses is the only effective policy for maintaining power, to which Darnay responds that their family has committed evil deeds and will pay for them. Darnay then renounces his property, position, and France as a whole, and Monseigneur ridicules Darnay for his lack of success in England. Monseigneur then mentions Dr. Manette and Lucie with an air of foreboding but refuses to elaborate.

Throughout the night, owls hoot and, as the sun rises, it makes the château's fountain look as if it is filled with blood. The poor villagers awaken first, going about their daily drudgery. Later, the residents of the château awaken and are suddenly frantic-- Monseigneur was murdered in the night. A knife through his heart has a note attached, which reads, "Drive him fast to his tomb. This, from Jacques."

Book II, Chapter 10

One year later, Darnay is happily living back in England, working as a French tutor. He works up the courage to tell Lucie of his long-standing love for her, and asks her father for permission. Dr. Manette is wary, but Darnay convinces him that his feelings are genuine and he only wants to add to their father-daughter relationship, not tear them apart.

Dr. Manette has long been reserved around Darnay and, although he gives his consent to Darnay, he still worries that something is off. Darnay tries to come clean with Dr. Manette--attempting to explain that he is living under an false name and why he is in England--but the doctor stops him before he can finish. Dr. Manette says that Darnay should wait until the morning after his marriage to Lucie to tell them all this, presuming the two do end up getting married. When Lucie returns to the house later in the day, she is confused and disturbed to hear her father working on his shoe-making again, which he has not done since he was in Paris. When she knocks on the door, he stops his work.

Thought Questions (students consider while they read)

1. What is the importance of Sydney Carton's willingness to step in for Charles Darnay at his trial, ensuring his acquittal on charges of espionage and treason?

2. What do you think the footsteps Lucie tells of hearing outside her door in Book II, Chapter 6 mean? How might these mysterious footsteps relate to broader themes in the novel?

3. What do we learn about the Marquis de Evrémonde--and the aristocracy more broadly--from the series of events that takes place during the Monseigneur's carriage ride in Book II, Chapters 7 & 8?

4. Describing the Marquis's château in the beginning of Book II, Chapter 9, Dickens writes:

   "It was a heavy mass of building, that chateau of Monsieur the Marquis, with a large stone court-yard before it, and two stone sweeps of staircase meeting in a stone terrace before the principal door. A stony business altogether with heavy stone balustrades...and stone faces of men, and stone heads of lions, in all directions. As if the Gorgon's head had surveyed it, when it was finished, two centuries ago." (119-120)

What linguistic and narrative devices does Dickens employ to suggest his feelings about the Marquis?

5. What is the significance of Dr. Manette's resumption of his shoemaking habit at the end of Book II, Chapter 10?

Vocabulary (in order of appearance)

"It was very small, very dark, very ugly, very incommodious." (II.1)

incommodious:

Uncomfortable, inconvenient, cramped.

"...with sufficient haste and trepidation to show that she was the person referred to." (II.1)

trepidation:

Fear, apprehension.

"...I'm as sleepy as laudanum, my lines is strained to that degree that I shouldn't know..." (II.1)

laudanum:

An alcoholic beverage containing morphine prepared from opium.

"...an aphorism that would be as final as it is lazy..." (II.2)

aphorism:

A pithy maxim or saying.

"Two gaolers, who had been standing there, went out, and the prisoner was brought in, and put to the bar." (II.2)

gaoler:

A jailer or prison guard.

"...and on the faith of his solemn asseveration that he already considered the prisoner as good as dead and gone." (II.3)

asseveration:

Affirmation or acknowledgement.

"Except that I remember them both to have been--like myself--timorous of highwaymen, and the prisoner has not a timorous air." (II.3)

timorous:

Showing anxiety or fear.

"'I'd hold half a guinea that he don't get no law-work to do.'" (II.3)

guinea:

An old British coin approximately equal to 1 pound and 1 shilling.

"...and the dismal place was deserted until to-morrow morning's interest of gallows, pillory, whipping post, and branding-iron..." (II.4)

pillory:

A wooden stock built to hold a prisoner's hands and head, usually in a public square to endure ridicule.

**"A slight frown and a laconic 'Yes,' were the answer."
(II.4)**

laconic:

Terse, succinct.

**"But it's not worth your while to apostrophise me, or the
air, about it..." (II.5)**

apostrophise:

A digression or address to someone who is not present.

**"...as a stake to speculate with, and had abandoned her
in her poverty for evermore, with no touch of
compunction." (II.6)**

compunction:

Guilt, misgivings, scruples.

**"Her dinners, of a very modest quality, were so well
cooked and so well served, and so neat in their
contrivances..." (II.6)**

contrivance:

Maneuvers, use of skills.

**"One lacquey carried the chocolate-pot into the sacred
presence..." (II.7)**

lacquey:

A servant or footman (archaic spelling).

"Deep would have been the blot upon his escutcheon if his chocolate hd been ignobly waited on by only three men..." (II.7)

escutcheon:

A coat of arms or family shield.

"...brazen ecclesiastics, of the worst world worldly, with sensual eyes, loose tongues, and looser lives..." (II.7)

ecclesiastic:

A clergy member or priest.

"'Your clemency, Monseigneur! He was not of this part of the country. Of all the days of my life I never saw him.'" (II.8)

clemency:

Leniency, mercy.

"...he had come out with great obsequiousness to assist at this examination..." (II.8)

obsequiousness:

Compliance or deference.

"The postilions, with a thousand gossamer gnats circling them in lieu of the Furies..." (II.8)

postilion:

Coach-man of a horse-drawn carriage.

"...in the next room (my bedroom), one fellow, to our knowledge, was poniarded on the spot for professing some insolent delicacy respecting his daughter..." (II.9)

poniarded:

Stabbed with a thin, small dagger.

Additional Homework

1. Following up on Day #2's activity on Poverty & Social Inequity in Late 18th and Early 19th Century England, re-read a short scene or chapter section from the readings so far that demonstrates some of the instances of poverty and social inequality in *A Tale of Two Cities*. Then, write a short response about how your perspective on this section has shifted or developed after conducting this research into the social conditions in Dickens's time.

2. Select the etching that goes along with one of the scenes read so far. Write a one-page analysis how the etching represents the different characters and events in the scene.

Day 2 - Discussion of Thought Questions

1. What is the importance of Sydney Carton's willingness to step in for Charles Darnay at his trial, ensuring his acquittal on charges of espionage and treason?

Time:

7-10 minutes

Discussion:

As a reminder, Charles Darnay's first trial is thrown into disarray when Mr. Carton--a man who looks almost identical to Darnay--reveals himself. In fact, while there is other evidence presented in Darnay's defense, Carton's appearance is the primary reason that Darnay is acquitted of the charges against him. This scene is yet another early instance of the theme of Doubles & Duality, which arises throughout the novel. Indeed, Dickens introduces the theme of Doubles & Duality beginning with the very title of the novel, *A Tale of Two Cities*. Indeed, most of the characters and settings in the novel come in pairs--London/Paris and Darnay/Carton, just to name a few examples--and are played off each other throughout the novel.

In addition, despite the early indications of Carton's licentious nature, this scene provides the first indication of his willingness to put himself on the line for a larger cause. Although Carton is explicit early on in his belief that his life is a waste and regularly makes a point to say that he does not truly care for anyone or anything, the reader senses that Carton actually subconsciously longs for a greater sense of purpose and meaning in his life. Even early on in the novel, just after Carton has helped to rescue Charles Darnay from conviction and execution, Carton cynical and sarcastic comments about Lucie show both his bitter personal biases as well as revealing his secret, developing feelings for Lucie Manette. This initial courtroom scene and Carton's subsequent conversation with Darnay lay the groundwork for the personal transformation that is to come in Carton's life, reinforcing the overarching themes of Resurrection and Sacrifice in *A Tale of Two Cities*.

2. What do you think the footsteps Lucie tells of hearing outside her door in Book II, Chapter 6 mean? How might these mysterious footsteps relate to broader themes in the novel?

Time:

7-10 minutes

Discussion:

Towards the end of the family's dinner party in Book II, Chapter 6, Lucie talks about her thinking of the footsteps she hears outside her house as those of people coming in and out of her life. Mr. Carton responds that this daydream may actually represent of the many people who are or will be part of her life. Although this is the first instance of this recurrent motif arising in the novel, students may recognize that the imagery seems to be foreshadowing greater ideas to come. Although this connection may seem tenuous at this point in the novel, more perceptive students may see the connection between these "footsteps" and the already frequently arising theme of Fate & The Passage of Time in *A Tale of Two Cities*.

Throughout the novel, Dickens frequently describes the passage of time and its connection to our fates as humans. Beginning in the very first chapter, with his references to trees awaiting their future as the guillotines of the French Revolution, Dickens suggests that this social movement was unavoidable. Indeed, Lucie's interpretation of the noise she keeps hearing of feet echoing through the halls draws upon the sense of inevitability associated with a Fate-driven universe. Throughout the novel, Dickens portrays Fate with a portentous tone rather than positive one. Although Lucie has a generally bright and optimistic outlook, her interpretation of the "footsteps" as suggesting that sometime in the future the past would come back to haunt them suggests the ways in which virtually all of the novel's characters sense the weighty inevitability of Fate in their lives.

3. What do we learn about the Marquis de Evrémonde--and the aristocracy more broadly--from the series of events that takes

place during the Monseigneur's carriage ride in Book II, Chapters 7 & 8?

Time:

7-10 minutes

Discussion:

Over the course of the Marquis de Evrémonde's carriage ride in these two chapters, Dickens manages to convey virtually every despicable quality associated with the corrupt and heartless aristocratic class in France leading up to the Revolution. Although the Marquis seems almost too ruthless and heartless to be believable as a true person, he is the ideal archetype of the brutality and corruption of the old social order in France. The Marquis's exploitation of and the disdain for the peasants in his area is especially obvious in his complete lack of empathy towards the father of the young boy his carriage tramples to death. The Marquis's behavior symbolizes the brutal aristocratic rule that the French peasants had had to endure for so long, and suggests Dickens's sympathy for the motivations of the revolutionaries.

More broadly, class struggle is an overriding theme throughout the novel, and this series of scenes is one of the first extended examples of the corruption and heartlessness of the aristocracy that laid the groundwork for the Revolution. Dickens clearly sympathizes with the motivations of the revolutionaries in France because of his own personal and political beliefs, which he demonstrates through his portrayal of the ruthlessness and cruelty of the aristocracy. Dickens clearly believes that there was significant justification for the peasants' desire for a societal overthrown.

4. Describing the Marquis's château in the beginning of Book II, Chapter 9, Dickens writes: "It was a heavy mass of building, that chateau of Monsieur the Marquis, with a large stone court-yard before it, and two stone sweeps of staircase meeting in a stone terrace before the principal door. A stony business altogether with heavy stone balustrades...and stone faces of men, and

stone heads of lions, in all directions. As if the Gorgon's head had surveyed it, when it was finished, two centuries ago." (119-120) What linguistic and narrative devices does Dickens employ to suggest his feelings about the Marquis?

Time:

7-10 minutes

Discussion:

Dickens's repetition of the word "stone" in this passage hints at the association he intends for the reader to draw between the cold stone forming the château's looming structure and the hardness of heart of the Marquis who resides there. In the previous few chapters, the reader witnesses the Marquis's complete misuse of his wealth and overindulgence in excessive luxuries coupled with his callous disregard for the poverty and suffering of the peasants in the villages surrounding his château. The Marquis's true nature is further reinforced by the cold and unfeeling stone building that has been in his family for generations.

In addition, Dickens's reference to Gorgon, who is one of the three sisters from Greek mythology whose hair is made of snakes and whose look turns one to stone, foreshadows the Marquis's imminent death. After the murder of the Marquis is discovered, the dead man's face is described as "like a fine mask, suddenly startled, made angry, and petrified. Driven home into the heart of the stone figure attached to it, with a knife" (130). This further reinforcement of the "stone" imagery suggests that the Marquis has now truly and fully turned to stone, becoming part of his family's long line of cold-hearted, ruthless aristocrats who abused their power. Furthermore, the Marquis's murder foreshadows the imminent overthrow of these upper classes as a result of the Revolution.

5. What is the significance of Dr. Manette's resumption of his shoemaking habit at the end of Book II, Chapter 10?

Time:

5-7 minutes

Discussion:

In order to better understand the significance of the ending of this chapter, students might need to review the other events leading up to it. A year after his trial and exoneration, Charles Darnay works up the courage to tell Lucie of his long-standing love for her, and asks her father for permission. Dr. Manette is wary, but Darnay convinces him that his feelings are genuine and he only wants to add to their father-daughter relationship, not tear them apart. Although Dr. Manette gives his consent to Darnay, he still worries that something is off. Darnay tries to come clean with Dr. Manette--attempting to explain that he is living under an false name and why he is in England--but the doctor stops him before he can finish. Dr. Manette says that Darnay should wait until the morning after his marriage to Lucie to tell them all this, presuming the two do end up getting married. When Lucie returns to the house later in the day, she is confused and disturbed to hear her father working on his shoe-making again, which he has not done since he was in Paris. When she knocks on the door, he stops his work.

Manette's resumption of his shoemaking--a coping mechanism of sorts that he picked up while imprisoned in the Bastille for so many years--foreshadows trouble to come for Darnay and the Manettes. Something about Darnay and his story to the Doctor has triggered some of the memories that Manette has suppressed since his time in prison. Although he does not yet know why he is wary of Darnay, the fact that he regresses into his shoemaking habit implies that there is some potential connection between Charles Darnay's secret past and Manette's time in prison.

Day 2 - Short Answer Evaluation

1.   What does Jerry Cruncher do for Tellson's bank?

   _____

2.   Who is on trial at the beginning of Book II?

   _____

3.   What is the name of Charles Darnay's look-alike, whose appearance throws
     his trial into disarray?

   _____

4.   Who is Mr. Stryver?

   _____

5.   What is the relationship between Mr. Stryver and Mr. Carton?

   _____

6.   Who is Miss Pross?

   _____

7.   What were the mysterious initials that Darnay recalls in his story about the
     Tower of London?

   _____

8.   What happens as a result of Monseigneur's carriage's reckless driving?

   _____

9. What does the scared villager say he saw on the Marquis's carriage?

_____

10. Who signed the note on the murdered Monseigneur's chest?

_____

Answer Key

1. He does whatever jobs they need him to do, which often seems to be the bank's dirty work.
2. Charles Darnay.
3. Mr. Carton.
4. Charles Darnay's lawyer.
5. Mr. Carton is Mr. Stryver's assistant, but they are also drinking partners and former classmates.
6. Lucie Manette's devoted maid.
7. D.I.G.
8. The carriage kills a child on the road through Saint Antoine.
9. A ghostly white, very tall man riding under the carriage.
10. Jacques.

Day 2 - Crossword Puzzle

ACROSS

1. The village through which the Marquis is riding.
4. Compliance or deference.
7. Charles _____ is on trial in Book II.
9. Terse, succinct.
12. Showing anxiety or fear.
16. Who signed the note stabbed into the Marquis's chest?
17. Uncomfortable, inconvenient.
18. A pithy maxim or saying.
20. Guilt, misgivings, scruples.

DOWN

2. Fear, apprehension.
3. Stabbed with a thin, small dagger.
5. Mr. _____ is the lawyer who wins the case.
6. Lucie's maid calls her "my _____."
8. Maneuvers, use of skills.
10. Charles's lawyer's assistant.
11. _____'s carriage kills a child.
13. Leniency, mercy.
14. Lucie's maid is Miss _____.
15. Cruncher and _____ both work for Tellson's.
19. Initials carved into a prison cell wall.

Crossword Puzzle Answer Key

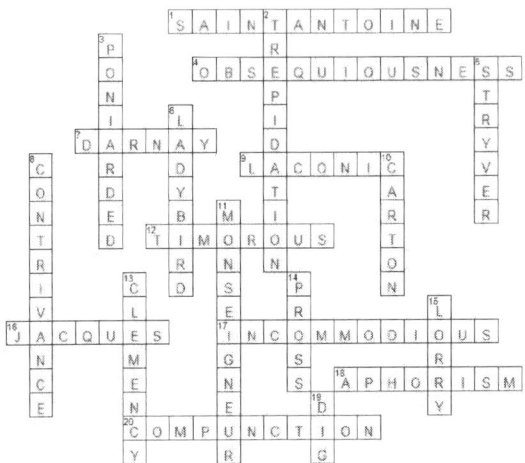

ACROSS

1. The village through which the Marquis is riding.
4. Compliance or deference.
7. Charles _____ is on trial in Book II.
9. Terse, succinct.
12. Showing anxiety or fear.
16. Who signed the note stabbed into the Marquis's chest?
17. Uncomfortable, inconvenient.
18. A pithy maxim or saying.
20. Guilt, misgivings, scruples.

DOWN

2. Fear, apprehension.
3. Stabbed with a thin, small dagger.
5. Mr. _____ is the lawyer who wins the case.
6. Lucie's maid calls her "my _____"
8. Maneuvers, use of skills.
10. Charles's lawyer's assistant.
11. _____'s carriage kills a child.
13. Leniency, mercy.
14. Lucie's maid is Miss _____
15. Cruncher and _____ both work for Tellson's.
19. Initials carved into a prison cell wall.

Day 2 - Vocabulary Quiz

Terms

1. _____ incommodious
2. _____ trepidation
3. _____ aphorism
4. _____ gaoler
5. _____ asserveration
6. _____ timorous
7. _____ laconic
8. _____ escutcheon
9. _____ clemency
10. _____ obsequiousness

Answers

A. A jailer or prison guard.
B. Compliance or deference.
C. Affirmation or acknowledgement.
D. A coat of arms or family shield.
E. Showing anxiety or fear.
F. Uncomfortable, inconvenient, cramped.
G. Fear, apprehension.
H. A pithy maxim or saying.
I. Terse, succinct.
J. Leniency, mercy.

Answer Key

1. F incommodious: Uncomfortable, inconvenient, cramped.
2. G trepidation: Fear, apprehension.
3. H aphorism: A pithy maxim or saying.
4. A gaoler: A jailer or prison guard.
5. C asserveration: Affirmation or acknowledgement.
6. E timorous: Showing anxiety or fear.
7. I laconic: Terse, succinct.
8. D escutcheon: A coat of arms or family shield.
9. J clemency: Leniency, mercy.
10. B obsequiousness: Compliance or deference.

Day 2 - Classroom Activities

1. The Life and Times of Charles Dickens

Kind of Activity:

Long-term Project

Objective:

Students will conduct research on life in late 18th and early 19th century England, examine how specific societal changes may have impacted Dickens's life and writings, and present their research and findings to the class.

Common Core Standards:

CCSS.ELA-Literacy.CCRA.R.4, CCSS.ELA-Literacy.CCRA.R.5

Time:

20-25 minutes (recurring)

Structure:

For an overview of this unit-long project, see the description in Day #1.

For Day #2, review the purpose of the activity and how it will continue through the unit. Then, demonstrate how to find important details from researching the world events and societal developments in England happening during Dickens's lifetime that could have impacted his perspectives about particular important themes in his writing. For example, identify the French Revolution and the rule of Queen Victoria as a significant cultural shift in England that impacted Dickens's and others' worldviews. Then identify a textual example of this theme arising in the Day #2 readings. Next, check for understanding, asking students questions about the observations and inferences made about the selected theme. Then, depending on student understanding, lead students in a guided practice--identifying another event or aspect of Dickens's life and a textual example of a related theme--or proceed to splitting students into groups.

Again, have the pre-assigned each group continue to research their assigned or selected theme. Again, themes might include: Science & Technology; Rebellions/

Revolutions in the late 18th and early 19th centuries; Queen Victoria's reign; Dickens's Religious Worldview/Outlook, Dickens's Literary & Philosophical influences; Literature in the Victorian era, Cultural/Religious Reactions to the French Revolution, etc.

Provide biographical sources on Dickens for students to read independently, or have them begin conducting their own research, depending on the time and resources available. These resources could include any of the following, in addition to many others:

Victorian England:

- http://www.english.uwosh.edu/roth/VictorianEngland.htm
- http://www.bbc.co.uk/history/british/victorians/
- http://www.aboutbritain.com/articles/victorian-era-1837-1901.asp
- https://www.wwnorton.com/college/english/nael/victorian/review/summary.htm
- http://www.history.ac.uk/ihr/Focus/Victorians/article.html
- https://www.history.org.uk/resources/primary_resource_3871_134.html

Charles Dickens:

- http://www.biography.com/people/charles-dickens-9274087
- http://www.bbc.co.uk/history/historic_figures/dickens_charles.shtml
- http://www.online-literature.com/dickens/
- http://www.britannica.com/biography/Charles-Dickens-British-novelist
- http://www.dickens-online.info/charles-dickens-biography.htm
- http://www.pbs.org/wgbh/masterpiece/dickens/dickens.html
- http://charlesdickenspage.com/
- http://dickensmuseum.com/
- http://dickenslive.com/
- http://www.dickensfellowship.org/life-charles-dickens

A Tale of Two Cities Analysis:

- http://www.gradesaver.com/tale-of-two-cities
- http://www.novelguide.com/a-tale-of-two-cities/theme-analysis
- http://www.litcharts.com/lit/a-tale-of-two-cities/plot-overview
- http://www.online-literature.com/dickens/twocities/
- http://charlesdickenspage.com/cities.html
- http://www.pbs.org/wgbh/masterpiece/archive/110/110.html

As in Day #1, the group scribe should chart the sociological events related to their group's theme, with a particular eye toward the ways that Day #2's readings have expanded their understanding of their assigned theme. Next, each group will examine the day's readings to find textual examples of the assigned theme. The group will then analyze their selected pieces of textual evidence and add them to their overall analysis.

Students will then share out one finding from their group with the whole class.

Ideas for Differentiated Instruction:

- Give students reading sections for research differentiated by reading level.
- Provide some groups with the option to read aloud the biographical section, or listen to/watch audio or video pieces about Dickens as a form of research.
- Assign students different roles—scribe, head researcher, lead note-taker, presenter, etc.—based on skills or areas for growth.
- Split students into groups by skill-set or areas of need, so that some groups can work more independently, and the teacher can support other groups more as needed.

Assessment Ideas:

- Student groups each generate a series of charts about an aspect of life or culture in Dickens's time and how it relates to his writings, with specific references to scenes from *A Tale of Two Cities*.
- Students present findings from group chart to the rest of the class.
- Students take notes, using an interactive handout (digital or paper), on other groups' theme presentations.
- Students present overall research and analysis at end of unit, using multimedia (audio/video/picture) presentations.

2. Evaluating Character in PBS Masterpiece's "A Tale of Two Cities"

Kind of Activity:

Group Work

Objective:

Students will watch the PBS Masterpiece's production of "A Tale of Two Cities," complete the Character Chart with known information thus far, discuss (in groups) how the Masterpiece portrayal of one of the characters differs from Dickens's version of that character, and present their findings to the class.

Common Core Standards:

CCSS.ELA-Literacy.CCRA.R.2, CCSS.ELA-Literacy.CCRA.R.4, CCSS.ELA-Literacy.CCRA.W.3, CCSS.ELA-Literacy.CCRA.SL.2

Time:

40-45 minutes

Structure:

For this activity, students can either watch Episode One of the PBS Masterpiece version of *A Tale of Two Cities* independently or as a class (see the website for the Masterpiece series here). In the DVD version, Episode One covers from the beginning of Disc One to the end of Chapter 6, which is approximately 54 minutes, and covers the content from the beginning of the novel through the end of Book the Second, Chapter 9 ("The Gorgon's Head").

Before watching the film, have students identify each of the novel's primary characters that has already been introduced, and lead a class discussion on important traits of the characters as portrayed in the novel as well as their relationships with other characters on the list. During and after watching the episode, students should complete as much as they can of the Character Chart found on page 24 of the PBS Masterpiece A Tale of Two Cities Teacher's Guide.

After students have watched the episode and fill out the chart, split students into small groups and assign each a character to analyze (or have the groups select their own characters). Next, have the small groups compare and contrast the novel version of the character with the miniseries version so far, and chart their comparisons. Then, have the groups present 2-3 points from their compare-and-contrast charts with the rest of the class.

Ideas for Differentiated Instruction:

- For the group section, split students into groups by skill-set or areas of need, so that some groups can work more independently, and the teacher can support other groups more (e.g. participating in the student discussion, helping to make connections, etc.).
- For the group section, assign students different roles—scribe, head researcher, lead note-taker, presenter, etc.—based on skills or areas for growth.
- For students who need additional support or ideas for how to fill out the chart and complete their character analyses, give students reading sections for research differentiated by reading level.

Assessment Ideas:

- Students individually complete the character chart and/or note-taking templates and submit for feedback.
- Student groups each generate a chart about their assigned *A Tale of Two Cities* character in the miniseries and connection to Dickens's portrayal of her.
- Students present findings from group chart to the rest of the class.

3. Poverty & Social Inequity in Late 18th and Early 19th Century England

Kind of Activity:

Research

Objective:

Students will research late 18th and early 19th century social issues and concerns in England, especially as related to children and poverty, and discuss how these social concerns may have impacted Dickens and his writings.

Common Core Standards:

CCSS.ELA-Literacy.CCRA.R.4, CCSS.ELA-Literacy.CCRA.R.6, CCSS.ELA-Literacy.CCRA.W.7, CCSS.ELA-Literacy.CCRA.W.8, CCSS.ELA-Literacy.CCRA.SL.4

Time:

30-35 minutes

Structure:

Begin by explaining that, from researching and reading about Dickens's life and beliefs, students know the social changes going on in England during his lifetime greatly impacted his perspectives on the world around him and his writing. In addition, from the chapters students have read so far, it is clear that some of the primary themes he grapples with include poverty and charity, child abandonment and child labor and, more broadly, the realities of human nature. In order to better understand the factors that shaped Dickens's complex perspectives on these themes, students will do station-based research on the factors that impacted Dickens's life and social issues and causes that shaped his writing.

Distribute a worksheet with designated areas for students to record reflections, evidence, and conclusions for each station. Next, explain the various stations to the students. Stations may vary substantially by class needs, as well as time and resources available, but could include:

- Image Analysis: Provide students with 4-5 images to examine and analyze from late 18th and early 19th century living conditions in England. For example, images from this history of poverty in England, from this BBC article about living conditions for the poor during Victorian times, or from this in-depth historical analysis of both images and writings from Dickens's time period.
- Film Excerpt Viewing: Excerpt a relevant section a film about poverty or child labor in late 18th and early 19th century England. For example, this short film has a number of interesting and relevant images (although they are dated somewhat later than Dickens's lifetime), this short film that shows interesting images and facts about child labor during this period, or this segment from a BBC documentary about child labor during the Industrial Revolution. Have students watch these excerpts to better understand the factors that may have impacted Dickens's worldview and perspectives on social issues in England.
- Literature Review: Provide students with 2-3 excerpts to read or skim from books that discuss the living conditions, poverty, and child labor issues during England's Industrial Revolution. A few examples of such books include: *Poverty and Poor Law Reform in Nineteenth Century Britain 1834-1914 - from Chadwick to Booth* by David Englander (Longman, 1998); *Report on the Sanitary Conditions of the Labouring Population of Great Britain* by Edwin Chadwick, 1842, ed. M.W. Flinn (1965); *The English Town* by Mark Girouard (Yale University Press, 1995); *State, Society and the Poor in Nineteenth Century England* by Alan Kidd, (Palgrave, 1999). These are only a few of the many articles and resources available, and they vary significantly in complexity and reading level, so may be used for different readers in the class.
- Reviewing Dickens's Journal Online: Select excerpts from Charles Dickens's numerous published works (available here) that best reflect his observations about and perspectives on the social issues and concerns of his time. Have students review and reflect on the journal pieces, and especially the relationship between Dickens's own personal perspectives and those of the characters in his writing.
- Independent Research: Give students access to computers or additional documents to facilitate their own independent research on late 18th and early 19th century perspectives around poverty, charity, and child labor.

After students have completed all of the stations, bring the class back together to discuss what they discovered, as well as any theories they have about how these factors may have impacted Dickens's life and writings.

Additional instructional resources for this activity can be found <u>here</u>.

Ideas for Differentiated Instruction:

- Provide various levels of scaffolding in the worksheets and charts distributed to students—some can have additional questions or sentence starters to get students thinking about the right themes, others can have challenge or in-depth thinking questions.
- At the literature review station, give several different lengths of excerpts (or varying reading levels) to give students options for what to analyze.

Assessment Ideas:

- The worksheet/chart that students fill in during the stations activity can be turned in as an assessment.
- Students can complete a final quiz or writing assignment at the end of class, drawing connections between the different stations, to be turned in for grading.

Day 3 - Reading Assignment, Questions, Vocabulary

Students read Book II, Chapters 11-21.

Common Core Objectives

- CCSS.ELA-Literacy.CCRA.R.2 Determine central ideas or themes of a text and analyze their development; summarize the key supporting details and ideas.

- CCSS.ELA-Literacy.CCRA.R.3 Analyze how and why individuals, events, or ideas develop and interact over the course of a text.

- CCSS.ELA-Literacy.CCRA.R.4 Interpret words and phrases as they are used in a text, including determining technical, connotative, and figurative meanings, and analyze how specific word choices shape meaning or tone.

- CCSS.ELA-Literacy.CCRA.R.6 Assess how point of view or purpose shapes the content and style of a text

- CCSS.ELA-Literacy.CCRA.R.9 Analyze how two or more texts address similar themes or topics in order to build knowledge or to compare the approaches the authors take.

- CCSS.ELA-Literacy.CCRA.W.3 Write narratives to develop real or imagined experiences or events using effective technique, well-chosen details and well-structured event sequences.

- CCSS.ELA-Literacy.CCRA.W.6 Use technology, including the Internet, to produce and publish writing and to interact and collaborate with others.

- CCSS.ELA-Literacy.CCRA.L.5 Demonstrate understanding of figurative language, word relationships, and nuances in word meanings.

- CCSS.ELA-Literacy.CCRA.SL.4 Present information, findings, and supporting evidence such that listeners can follow the line of reasoning and the organization, development, and style are appropriate to task, purpose, and audience.

Note that it is perfectly fine to expand any day's work into two days depending on the characteristics of the class, particularly if the class will engage in all of the suggested classroom exercises and activities and discuss all of the thought questions.

Content Summary for Teachers

Book II, Chapter 11

Mr. Stryver and Mr. Carton are drinking together again. Explaining that he is more honorable than Carton, Stryver says that he plans to marry Lucie Manette. Although Carton says he's fine with this arrangement, he begins to drink much more rapidly. Stryver believes he is doing a noble deed in marrying Lucie, marveling at his own willingness to make a financial sacrifice in pursuing the match. Stryver suggests that Carton should find a wealthy or propertied woman to marry.

Book II, Chapter 12

On his way to the Manette residence, Mr. Stryver stops by Tellson's back to ask Mr. Lorry's opinion on his impending proposal to Lucie. Lorry expresses consternation about this idea, and Stryver asks what's wrong. Stryver notes that he is an eligible bachelor with promising prospects and says that Lucie would be foolish to refuse him.

Mr. Lorry becomes upset with Mr. Stryver for his unkind words about Lucie. Lorry suggests that he go assess the viability of Stryver's possible proposal with the Manettes before the Stryver himself attempts it. Stryver accepts this idea.

Later in the evening, Lorry goes to Stryver's home to tell him that, as he had thought might be the case, a proposal from Stryver would be a bad idea. Weirdly, Stryver pretends to have forgotten the idea. When Lorry reminds him of their earlier conversation, Stryver suggests that Lucie has gotten into trouble and is no longer a lady worthy of engagement. Lorry leaves, baffled.

Book II, Chapter 13

Although he has never seemed to like the Manettes, nor they him, Mr. Carton has often wandered their street at night, thinking about Lucie. Carton visits the Manette home one day and tells Lucie that their happy family has made him want to reform his wayward life, although he thinks he may be beyond help at this point. Lucie attempts to persuade Carton that his dream is possible, but Carton insists that it's only a happy fantasy. Carton then says that he only wanted to tell her his true feelings. Then, Carton tells Lucie that he would do anything to help her or her close family and friends.

Book II, Chapter 14

Jerry Cruncher sits outside Tellson's on Fleet Street and watches as Robert Cly's funeral procession passes by. An angry crowd follows behind the processional, because Cly was supposedly a spy. Jerry joins the mob, but leaves before the police arrive.

Jerry returns home to find Mrs. Cruncher praying again. He lectures her and then, late at night, says he's going out fishing. Cruncher's son, young Jerry, follows him and watches as his father goes own to the river and opens a coffin. Alarmed, young Jerry rushes home, thinking the coffin is chasing him. In the morning, young Jerry asks Cruncher about a Resurrection-Man. His father is happy to hear that young Jerry would like to be one when he grows up.

Book II, Chapter 15

Back at Monsieur Defarges' wine-shop, Defarge comes in with a road-mender named Jacques. Defarge takes Jacques up to Dr. Manette's former apartment and introduces him to the other three Jacques. The new Jacques tells the others of seeing the ghostly man hanging beneath Monseigneur's carriage. He claims he recognized him again later because of his height when he saw him being led away by soldiers; in addition, he says the tall man seemed to recognize him as well. The tall man is in prison for the alleged murder of Monseigneur and gallows have been built for his execution.

After the new Jacques leaves, Defarge discusses his story with the other three Jacques. They talk about the tall man's fate. One of the Jacques is concerned about whether their secret information is safe, which Defarge assures them it is as his wife knits it in secret symbols that she alone can decipher. The Defarges bring the new Jacques to see Versailles where he calls out to the aristocrats. Madame Defarge tells an inquiring man that she is knitting shrouds. As they leave, the Defarges discuss their disdain for the aristocrats and royalty.

Book II, Chapter 16

Monsieur Defarge learns from a policeman that an English spy named John Barsad is in Saint Antoine and gets a description of the man. Returning to their wine-shop, the Defarges count their money. Monsieur Defarge is worn out, and Madame Defarge tries to reassure him that although they may not get to see a revolution during their lives, they can help prepare for it.

The following day, Barsad enters the shop and Madame Defarge recognizes him. She put a rose in her hair and everyone else leaves the wine-shop. Barsad attempts to entrap Madame Defarge into complaining about Gaspard's execution or the social inequity in France. From this conversation, Madame Defarge learns that Gaspard is the imprisoned man who the road-mender Jacques told them about. When Monsieur Defarge enters the shop, he confirms Madame Defarge's claim that the village does not sympathize with Gaspard. Barsad tries to get the Defarges to crack by telling them he knows about Dr. Manette and informing them that Lucie has married Darnay. He tells them that Darnay is the Monseigneur's nephew and so has become the new Marquis. The Defarges pretend to be unmoved by this new information, and Barsad leaves.

Book II, Chaper 17

Dr. Manette reassures Lucie that pursuing her own happiness with Darnay will not harm his and Lucie's relationship. He also tells her that when he was imprisoned, he would often daydream about her remembering him. Lucie responds that she often thought about him through her entire childhood.

The wedding is an intimate gathering with Miss Pross and Mr. Lorry as the only guests. Lucie continues to worry about her father, but when she goes to make sure he is okay during the night she finds him sleeping soundly.

Book II, Chapter 18

Although the wedding is a happy occasion, Miss Pross remains convinced that her brother should have been the one marrying Miss Manette. Mr. Lorry also makes advances towards Lucie, wondering if he should've gotten married, rather than remaining a bachelor.

Darnay reveals his true identity to Dr. Manette, but Lucie and Darnay do indeed get married. When the couple leaves for their honeymoon to Wales, Dr. Manette regresses back to his habits from prison, starting to make shoes again, and is unable to recognize Miss Pross. Mr. Lorry and Miss Pross don't tell Lucie of the change, but just keep an eye on Dr. Manette at all hours to make sure he does not deteriorate further.

Book II, Chapter 19

On the morning the couple is supposed to return from their honeymoon, Dr. Manette has returned to normal. Miss Pross and Mr. Lorry act like nothing strange has happened, but Lorry decides to present the "case" to Dr. Manette as if it was another "patient." Manette understands that he had been the one making shoes, and says that his equipment should be secretly taken away from him to prevent him from doing so in the future. Manette also tells Lorry that he has no memory of the regression and thinks he should just continue about his normal activities as if nothing happened.

Later, Lorry and Pross completely destroy the shoemaking equipment while Dr. Manette is out visiting Lucie and Mr. Darnay.

Book II, Chapter 20

Upon returning from their honeymoon, Mr. Carton is the first person to greet Mr. Darnay and Lucie. Carton says he wants to make amends with Darnay for any prior ill feelings he expressed towards him. Darnay tells Carton that he did more than enough by helping to save his life when he was on trial, and that he's welcome at their home anytime.

After Carton departs, Darnay tells Lucie about their conversation, noting what a strange and mysterious man Carton is. Although Darnay doesn't mean to be hurtful, Lucie is troubled by his words and asks him to be more empathetic towards Carton.

Book II, Chapter 21

As Lucie gets older, footsteps continue to echo throughout the house. She gives birth to a baby boy who dies young and then a little girl who is also named Lucie. Carton remains an important part of the Darnay family. Stryver marries a rich widow and tries to have Darnay take the widow's children on as students. When Darnay turns him down, Stryver is offended.

In 1789, when little Lucie is six years hold, events start to unfold in France that affect the Darnay household. Mr. Lorry notes that many customers of Tellson's in Paris are so worried about what is brewing in France that they're moving all their money to the London. He worries for little Lucie, and then wonders why he is so nervous. In the meantime, the storming of the Bastille is approaching, and the citizens of Saint Antoine arm themselves with anything they can find for weapons. The Defarges lead the citizens of Saint Antoine in the attack. Monsieur Defarge finds Dr. Manette's former cell and removes a document from its secret hiding place before the destruction of the Bastille.

When Defarge returns to the mob, they are about to execute the governor. Madame Defarge waits for the mob to beat the governor to death before mutilating the body. The mob releases seven prisoners from the Bastille, hailing them as heroes.

Thought Questions (students consider while they read)

1. What does Book II, Chapter 11 reveal about Mr. Stryver and Mr. Carton's characters?

2. Over the course of Book II, a complex love quadrilateral develops between Lucie Manette and Darnay, Stryver, and Carton. What is the significance of this complicated romantic situation and how does it reflect and impact the different characters involved?

3. What new information do we learn about Jerry Cruncher in Book II, Chapter 14? How does this discovery relate to broader themes in the novel at this stage?

4. What is the significance of Madame Defarge's knitting in Book II, Chapter 15?

5. Why do you think Dr. Manette regresses again, going back to his shoemaking, after Lucie and Charles Darnay go off on their honeymoon? What do we learn about Dr. Manette's character from these instances?

Vocabulary (in order of appearance)

"Mr. Stryver having made up his mind to that magnanimous betstowal of good fortune on the Doctor's daughter..." (II.12)

magnanimous:

Generous, benevolent, charitable.

"He shook in a self-abnegating way, as one who shook for Tellson and Co." (II.12)

abnegating:

Rejecting or renouncing something cherished or valuable.

"Having supposed that there was sense where there is no sense, and a laudable ambition where there is not a laudable ambition..." (II.12)

laudable:

Praise-worthy, admirable.

"'What are you hooroaring at?'" (II.14)

hooroaring:

Shouting, yelling.

"...clapping his hands to his mouth nevertheless, and vociferating in a surprising heat and with the greatest ardour..." (II.14)

vociferating:

Yelling, arguing.

"Having smoked his pipe out, and ruminated a little longer..." (II.14)

ruminate:

Contemplate, think about, consider deeply.

"'If, as an honest tradesman, my wenturs goes wrong to-night...'" (II.14)

wenturs:

Ventures, adventures (old British slang).

"Look at your boy: he is you'rn, ain't he? He's a thin as a lath." (II.14)

lath:

A skinny, flat strip of wood.

"Thus, Saint Antoine in this vinous feature of his, until mid-day." (II.14)

vinous:

Demonstrating the effects of drinking wine.

"The mender of the roads, blue cap in hand, wiped his swarthy forehead with it..." (II.14)

swarthy:

Tanned, dark-skinned.

"...because Monseigneur was the father of his tenants--serfs--what you will--he will be executed as a parricide." (II.15)

parricide:

Killing of one's parent or other close relative.

"...as if he had never of ubiquitous Jacques in his time." (II.15)

ubiquitous:

Omnipresent, all over the place.

"nose aquiline, but not straight, having a peculiar inclination towards the left cheek..." (II.16)

aquiline:

Curved or bent.

"Next noontide saw the admirable woman in her usual place in the wine-shop, knitting away assiduously." (II.16)

assiduously :

Unceasingly, constantly.

"He only seemed to contrast his present cheerfulness and felicity with the dire endurance that was over." (II.17)

felicity:

Joy, immense happiness.

"...I had no intention of rendering those trifling articles of remembrance..." (II.18)

trifling:

Trivial, insignificant.

"He spoke with the diffidence of a man who knew how slight a thing would overset the delicate organisation of the mind..." (II.19)

diffidence:

Modesty, meekness.

"'You see too,' said the Doctor, tremulously, 'it is such an old companion.'" (II.19)

tremulously:

Fearfully, timidly.

"If one forlorn wanderer then pacing the dark streets..." (II.20)

forlorn:

Miserable, unhappy.

"...which is surely such an incorrigible aggravation of an originally bad offence..." (II.21)

incorrigible:

Habitual, confirmed.

Additional Homework

1. Complete a close analysis of one of the scenes in the novel not discussed in class, making sure to note and label the different aspects of character, structure, language and imagery, and voice and characters.

2. As an extension of today's classroom activity about the French Revolution, write a 2-3 page history of the lead-up to the Revolution, the events themselves, and the aftermath. Be sure to cite at least 3 relevant historical sources in your short paper.

Day 3 - Discussion of Thought Questions

1. What does Book II, Chapter 11 reveal about Mr. Stryver and Mr. Carton's characters?

Time:

7-10 minutes

Discussion:

In this chapter, Mr. Stryver and Mr. Carton are drinking together again. Explaining that he is more honorable than Carton, Stryver says that he plans to marry Lucie Manette. Although Carton says he's fine with this arrangement, he begins to drink much more rapidly. Stryver believes he is doing a noble deed in marrying Lucie, marveling at his own willingness to make a financial sacrifice in pursuing the match. Stryver suggests that Carton should find a wealthy or propertied woman to marry.

This chapter reveals to readers what a tremendously pompous and prideful man Stryver is. In his conversation with Carton, he clearly assumes that Lucie Manette will gladly accept his offer of marriage, because he believes himself to be such an eligible bachelor. Furthermore, Stryver's insistence on his own selflessness in marrying someone poorer than himself adds to the self-satisfied pompousness he exudes in this scene. This chapter also sets up the complicated love quadrilateral between Lucie Manette and Darnay, Stryver, and Carton, which will play out in the subsequent several chapters.

2. Over the course of Book II, a complex love quadrilateral develops between Lucie Manette and Darnay, Stryver, and Carton. What is the significance of this complicated romantic situation and how does it reflect

and impact the different characters involved?

Time:

7-10 minutes

Discussion:

Over the course of a number of chapters in Book II, beginning around Chapter 5 but really picking up in Chapter 10, a complex romantic situation develops in which virtually every man who encounters Lucie Manette seems to fall in love with her. Charles Darnay is humble and earnest in expressing his emotions, and seems to genuinely want to marry Lucie out of true love for her. In contrast, Mr. Stryver's affection for Lucie comes off as very self-serving--he assumes she will welcome his advances and commends himself for his willing self-sacrifice in marrying for "love" rather than money. Finally, Sydney Carton keeps his feelings for Lucie secret--his romantic attraction to her is heavily wrapped up in his own feelings of self-doubt and worthlessness, which makes it very hard for him to admit how he truly feels, even to himself. Despite his hesitancy, Carton's love for Lucie is actually the catalyst for immense transformation in his life. Although he initially dismisses his romantic feelings as completely unrealistic, he is eventually able to profess his love to her directly. Not surprisingly, Lucie goes on to marry Darnay anyway, and Carton persists in believing himself to be a worthless human being, but this scene marks a turning point in Carton's life.

More broadly, Lucie's role in all of these different men's lives suggests her connective role in the story overall. In other words, many important plot developments take place over the course of this Book and Lucie is directly or indirectly connected to virtually all of them. Indeed, it is Lucie who connects Sydney Carton to Charles Darnay, Darnay to Doctor Manette, and Mr. Lorry to the family more broadly, and she is the motivation for many of the men in the story to pursue a greater purpose in their lives. As a result, the complicated feelings that so many individuals develop towards Lucie over the course of this Book simply serve to further reinforce her significance as a crucial character who binds others together.

3. What new information do we learn about Jerry Cruncher in Book II, Chapter 14? How does this discovery relate to broader themes in the novel at this stage?

Time:

7-10 minutes

Discussion:

In this chapter, after watching Roger Cly's funeral procession and briefly joining the following angry mob, Jerry returns home to find Mrs. Cruncher praying again. He lectures her and then, late at night, says he's going out fishing. Cruncher's son, young Jerry, follows him and watches as his father goes own to the river and opens a coffin. Alarmed, young Jerry rushes home, thinking the coffin is chasing him. In the morning, young Jerry asks Cruncher about a Resurrection-Man. His father is happy to hear that young Jerry would like to be one when he grows up.

This revelation about the true nature of Cruncher's unsavory side-job as a "Resurrection-Man"--which deals primarily with grave-robbing and selling body parts for profit--is a darkly humorous iteration of the recurrent theme of Resurrection in the novel. Interestingly, despite the unpleasant nature of Cruncher's occupation, it leads him to the discovery of Roger Cly's empty grave--showing that the spy never actually died as everyone had thought. By having Cruncher use his secret profession to discover such important information that serves the greater good, Dickens is also reinforcing the idea that even the poor and downcast have an important part to play in society.

4. What is the significance of Madame Defarge's knitting in Book II, Chapter 15?

Time:

7-10 minutes

Discussion:

This is the first time the reader gets more information about Madame Defarge's knitting and it tells us a lot about Madame Defarge's broader character. In this chapter, we learn that Madame Defarge uses actual symbols in her knitting to communicate with other members of the revolutionary movement (the symbols list names of those who would be condemned to death when the new revolutionary regime came to power). The knitting itself and the purpose behind it serves as a metaphor as well, however, of Madame Defarge's vengeful, malicious nature and, more broadly, the cunning and cold-blooded brutality of all the revolutionaries. Although Madame Defarge appears to be picture of calm, domestic femininity as she knits, she is actually sentencing her enemies to death. In a similar fashion, the impoverished and pitiable French peasants soon prove to be just as brutal and blindly violent as their former aristocratic oppressors. Significantly, Dickens's use of knitting imagery evokes the knitting and weaving traditionally associated with Fate in classical mythology, suggesting the inextricable link between vindictiveness and fate in the novel. Furthermore, Dickens's heavy reliance on this symbol suggests the timelessness of this tale throughout human history and the cyclical nature of fate and human destiny.

5. Why do you think Dr. Manette regresses again, going back to his shoemaking, after Lucie and Charles Darnay go off on their honeymoon? What do we learn about Dr. Manette's character from these instances?

Time:

7-10 minutes

Discussion:

In Book II, Chapter 18, Darnay reveals his true identity to Dr. Manette, but Lucie and Darnay do indeed get married as planned. However, revealing his underlying anxieties about Darnay, when the couple leaves for their honeymoon to Wales, Dr. Manette regresses back to his habits from prison, starting to make shoes again, and is unable to recognize Miss Pross. Mr. Lorry and Miss Pross don't tell Lucie of the change, but just keep an eye on Dr. Manette at all hours to make sure he does not deteriorate further. Interestingly, by the morning that Lucie and Darnay are supposed to return from their honeymoon in Book II, Chapter 19, Dr. Manette has returned to normal. Miss Pross and Mr. Lorry act like nothing strange has happened, but Lorry decides to present the "case" to Dr. Manette as if it was another "patient." Manette understands that he had been the one making shoes, and says that his equipment should be secretly taken away from him to prevent him from doing so in the future. Manette also tells Lorry that he has no memory of the regression and thinks he should just continue about his normal activities as if nothing happened. Later, Lorry and Pross completely destroy the shoemaking equipment while Dr. Manette is out visiting Lucie and Mr. Darnay.

This whole series of events gives the reader a fascinating insight into Dr. Manette as a character and his broader role in the novel. Moreover, readers can learn a great deal about Dickens's rather progressive understanding of human nature and the human psyche. Despite all he has suffered, Dickens shows Manette as undergoing a massive transformation over the course of the novel. He begins the novel as a broken man who has been thoroughly traumatized by his lengthy imprisonment. After his release from jail, the meaningful experiences and loving relationships that Manette enjoys over the course of the novel strengthen him and bring him (figuratively) back to life. Although this transformation of Manette's character, caused by the experiences and relationships in his life, may not seem all that notable to modern readers, the idea Dickens suggests through this change--that people's surroundings and experiences can impact their lives and identities--was actually quite revolutionary in his time. In addition, Manette's ability to transform himself from damaged former prisoner into strong and dedicated family patriarch reinforces the theme of Resurrection that permeates the novel.

Day 3 - Short Answer Evaluation

1. What kind of woman does Mr. Stryver suggest Mr. Carton should try to find to marry?

   _____

2. Whose opinion does Mr. Stryver ask about his plan to propose to Lucie Manette?

   _____

3. What does Mr. Carton tell Lucie when he visits the Manettes?

   _____

4. What activity does Mr. Cruncher reprimand Mrs. Cruncher for?

   _____

5. What does Madame Defarge claim she is knitting?

   _____

6. How does Madame Defarge signal that she needs people to leave the shop?

   _____

7. Who is John Barsad?

   _____

8. What happens to Dr. Manette when Lucie and Charles Darnay go on their honeymoon?

   _____

9. How does Dr. Manette suggest preventing himself from making shoes in the future?

_____

10. What year does the novel move forward to in Book II, Chapter 21?

_____

Answer Key

1. A wealthy or propertied woman.
2. Mr. Lorry.
3. Mr. Carton tells Lucie that the Manette's happy family has made him want to reform his wayward life.
4. Praying.
5. Shrouds.
6. She puts a rose in her hair.
7. An English spy.
8. He regresses back to his habits from prison, starting to make shoes again, and is unable to recognize Miss Pross.
9. He suggests that the equipment should be secretly taken away from him.
10. 1789.

Day 3 - Crossword Puzzle

ACROSS
2. Omnipresent, all over the place.
4. Stryver wants to marry _____.
5. Praise-worthy, admirable.
6. Joy, immense happiness.
8. Trivial, insignificant.
12. Where the Darnays go on their honeymoon.
14. The French _____ begins in 1789.
16. Curved or bent.
17. Cruncher's secret profession: _____ Man.
19. Unceasingly, constantly.
20. The true English spy.

DOWN
1. Contemplate, think about.
3. Madame Defarge knits _____ into her creations.
7. Cruncher reprimands his wife for _____.
9. Defarge puts a _____ in her hair to signal she needs privacy.
10. Generous, benevolent, charitable.
11. Madame Defarge claims she's knitting _____.
13. Miserable, unhappy.
15. Tanned, dark-skinned.
18. Where the Manettes live in London.

Crossword Puzzle Answer Key

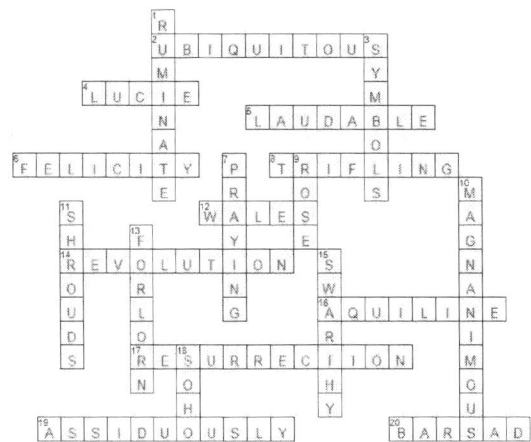

ACROSS

2. Omnipresent, all over the place.
4. Stryver wants to marry _____.
5. Praise-worthy, admirable.
6. Joy, immense happiness.
8. Trivial, insignificant.
12. Where the Darnays go on their honeymoon.
14. The French _____ begins in 1789.
16. Curved or bent.
17. Cruncher's secret profession: _____ Man.
19. Unceasingly, constantly.
20. The true English spy.

DOWN

1. Contemplate, think about.
3. Madame Defarge knits _____ into her creations.
7. Cruncher reprimands his wife for _____.
9. Defarge puts a _____ in her hair to signal she needs privacy.
10. Generous, benevolent, charitable.
11. Madame Defarge claims she's knitting _____.
13. Miserable, unhappy.
15. Tanned, dark-skinned.
18. Where the Manettes live in London.

Day 3 - Vocabulary Quiz

Terms

1. _____ magnanimous
2. _____ laudable
3. _____ vociferating
4. _____ ruminate
5. _____ vinous
6. _____ swarthy
7. _____ ubiquitous
8. _____ aquiline
9. _____ assiduously
10. _____ trifling

Answers

A. Praise-worthy, admirable.
B. Yelling, arguing.
C. Unceasingly, constantly.
D. Contemplate, think about, consider deeply.
E. Curved or bent.
F. Demonstrating the effects of drinking wine.
G. Generous, benevolent, charitable.
H. Tanned, dark-skinned.
I. Trivial, insignificant.
J. Omnipresent, all over the place.

Answer Key

1. G magnanimous: Generous, benevolent, charitable.
2. A laudable: Praise-worthy, admirable.
3. B vociferating: Yelling, arguing.
4. D ruminate: Contemplate, think about, consider deeply.
5. F vinous: Demonstrating the effects of drinking wine.
6. H swarthy: Tanned, dark-skinned.
7. J ubiquitous: Omnipresent, all over the place.
8. E aquiline: Curved or bent.
9. C assiduously: Unceasingly, constantly.
10. I trifling: Trivial, insignificant.

Day 3 - Classroom Activities

1. The Life and Times of Charles Dickens

Kind of Activity:

Long-term Project

Objective:

Students will conduct research on life in late 18th and early 19th century England, examine how specific societal changes may have impacted Dickens's life and writings, and present their research and findings to the class.

Common Core Standards:

CCSS.ELA-Literacy.CCRA.R.4, CCSS.ELA-Literacy.CCRA.R.5

Time:

20-25 minutes (recurring)

Structure:

For an overview of this unit-long project, see the description in Day #1.

For Day #3, review the purpose of the activity and how it will continue through the unit. Then, demonstrate how to find important details from researching the world events and societal developments in England happening during Dickens's lifetime that could have impacted his perspectives about particular important themes in his writing. For example, identify the French Revolution and the rule of Queen Victoria as a significant cultural shift in England that impacted Dickens's and others' worldviews. Then identify a textual example of this theme arising in the Day #3 readings. Next, check for understanding, asking students questions about the observations and inferences made about the selected theme. Then, depending on student understanding, lead students in a guided practice--identifying another event or aspect of Dickens's life and a textual example of a related theme--or proceed to splitting students into groups.

As in previous days of this activity, have the pre-assigned each group continue to research their assigned or selected theme. As mentioned previously, themes might include: Science & Technology; Rebellions/Revolutions in the late 18th and early 19th centuries; Queen Victoria's reign; Dickens's Religious Worldview/Outlook, Dickens's Literary & Philosophical influences; Literature in the Victorian era, Cultural/Religious Reactions to the French Revolution, etc.

Provide biographical sources on Dickens for students to read independently, or have them begin conducting their own research, depending on the time and resources available. These resources could include any of the following, in addition to many others:

Victorian England:

- http://www.english.uwosh.edu/roth/VictorianEngland.htm
- http://www.bbc.co.uk/history/british/victorians/
- http://www.aboutbritain.com/articles/victorian-era-1837-1901.asp
- https://www.wwnorton.com/college/english/nael/victorian/review/summary.htm
- http://www.history.ac.uk/ihr/Focus/Victorians/article.html
- https://www.history.org.uk/resources/primary_resource_3871_134.html

Charles Dickens:

- http://www.biography.com/people/charles-dickens-9274087
- http://www.bbc.co.uk/history/historic_figures/dickens_charles.shtml
- http://www.online-literature.com/dickens/
- http://www.britannica.com/biography/Charles-Dickens-British-novelist
- http://www.dickens-online.info/charles-dickens-biography.htm
- http://www.pbs.org/wgbh/masterpiece/dickens/dickens.html
- http://charlesdickenspage.com/
- http://dickensmuseum.com/
- http://dickenslive.com/
- http://www.dickensfellowship.org/life-charles-dickens

A Tale of Two Cities Analysis:

- http://www.gradesaver.com/tale-of-two-cities
- http://www.novelguide.com/a-tale-of-two-cities/theme-analysis
- http://www.litcharts.com/lit/a-tale-of-two-cities/plot-overview
- http://www.online-literature.com/dickens/twocities/
- http://charlesdickenspage.com/cities.html
- http://www.pbs.org/wgbh/masterpiece/archive/110/110.html

As in Days #1 & 2, the group scribe should chart the sociological events related to their group's theme, with a particular eye toward the ways that Day #3's readings have expanded their understanding of their assigned theme. Next, each group will examine the day's readings to find textual examples of the assigned theme. The group will then analyze their selected pieces of textual evidence and add them to their overall analysis.

Students will then share out one finding from their group with the whole class.

Ideas for Differentiated Instruction:

- Give students reading sections for research differentiated by reading level.
- Provide some groups with the option to read aloud the biographical section, or listen to/watch audio or video pieces about Dickens as a form of research.
- Assign students different roles—scribe, head researcher, lead note-taker, presenter, etc.—based on skills or areas for growth.
- Split students into groups by skill-set or areas of need, so that some groups can work more independently, and the teacher can support other groups more as needed.

Assessment Ideas:

- Student groups each generate a series of charts about an aspect of life or culture in Dickens's time and how it relates to his writings, with specific references to scenes from *A Tale of Two Cities*.
- Students present findings from group chart to the rest of the class.
- Students take notes, using an interactive handout (digital or paper), on other groups' theme presentations.
- Students present overall research and analysis at end of unit, using multimedia (audio/video/picture) presentations.

2. Researching the Revolution

Kind of Activity:

Research

Objective:

Students will research the events surrounding the French Revolution, and discuss how these events may have impacted events in England, as well as Dickens and his writings.

Common Core Standards:

CCSS.ELA-Literacy.CCRA.R.4, CCSS.ELA-Literacy.CCRA.R.6, CCSS.ELA-Literacy.CCRA.W.7, CCSS.ELA-Literacy.CCRA.W.8, CCSS.ELA-Literacy.CCRA.SL.4

Time:

30-35 minutes

Structure:

From researching and reading about Dickens's life and events in England at the time, students know the social changes going on in France and England during Dickens's lifetime greatly impacted his perspectives on the world around him and his writing. In addition, from reading the preface and the chapters so far, students can see that Dickens has complex perspectives on the French Revolution and its implications for France, England, and people of many different social classes. In order to better understand the real history underlying *A Tale of Two Cities,* students will do individual and/or small group research on The French Revolution.

Distribute a worksheet with designated areas for students to record reflections, evidence, and conclusions for each station. Next, explain the various stations to the students. Stations may vary substantially by class needs, as well as time and resources available, but could include:

The French Revolution:

- http://www.history.com/topics/french-revolution
- http://www.britannica.com/event/French-Revolution
- http://www.historytoday.com/maurice-cranston/french-revolution-ideas-and-ideologies
- http://www.eyewitnesstohistory.com/frenchrevolution.htm
- https://history.state.gov/milestones/1784-1800/french-rev
- https://www.youtube.com/watch?v=SyXcUMftRs8

Impact of the French Revolution in England:

- http://www.bl.uk/romantics-and-victorians/articles/the-impact-of-the-french-revolution-in-britain
- http://www.nationalarchives.gov.uk/pathways/citizenship/struggle_democracy/revolution.htm
- http://www.bbc.co.uk/history/british/empire_seapower/british_french_rev_01.shtml
- http://crossref-it.info/articles/178/impact-of-the-french-revolution
- http://www.historyhome.co.uk/c-eight/france/impactfr.htm

Victorian England:

- http://www.english.uwosh.edu/roth/VictorianEngland.htm
- http://www.bbc.co.uk/history/british/victorians/
- http://www.aboutbritain.com/articles/victorian-era-1837-1901.asp

- https://www.wwnorton.com/college/english/nael/victorian/review/summary.htm
- http://www.history.ac.uk/ihr/Focus/Victorians/article.html
- https://www.history.org.uk/resources/primary_resource_3871_134.html

After students have completed their own independent or small group research, bring the class back together to discuss what they discovered, as well as any theories they have about how these factors may have impacted Dickens's life and writings.

Additional instructional resources for this activity can be found here.

Ideas for Differentiated Instruction:

- Provide various levels of scaffolding in the worksheets and charts distributed to students—some can have additional questions or sentence starters to get students thinking about the right themes, others can have challenge or in-depth thinking questions.
- Give students reading sections for research differentiated by reading level.
- Provide some groups with the option to read aloud the biographical section, or listen to/watch audio or video pieces about Dickens as a form of research.

Assessment Ideas:

- The worksheet/chart that students fill in during the stations activity can be turned in as an assessment.
- Students can complete a final quiz or writing assignment at the end of class, drawing connections between the different stations, to be turned in for grading.

3. Acting out Scenes from "A Tale of Two Cities"

Kind of Activity:

Performance

Objective:

Students will analyze the dramatic elements from Book I, Chapter 1 through Book II, Chapter 21, interpret the scenes into something that can be performed, perform their interpretations of the selected scenes, and watch and evaluate other groups' performances

Common Core Standards:

CCSS.ELA-Literacy.CCRA.R.1, CCSS.ELA-Literacy.CCRA.R.4, CCSS.ELA-Literacy.CCRA.R.5, CCSS.ELA-Literacy.CCRA.SL.6

Time:

30-35 minutes

Structure:

Prior to class, select 4-5 short scenes from any of the chapters read so far in *A Tale of Two Cities* that can be easily performed. A few options include:

- The scene in Book I, Chapter 2 in which Mr. Cruncher brings Mr. Lorry a letter on the ride to Dover.
- The scene in which Lucie comes to rescue her father from the wine-shop apartment in Book I, Chapters 5-6.
- The courtroom scene in Book II, Chapters 2-3.
- The dinner party at the Manettes' house in Book II, Chapter 6.
- Sections from the series of events during the Monseigneur's ride through the country in Book II, Chapters 7-9.
- The scene with the Defarges and their friends in the wine-shop in Book II, Chapter 15-16.
- Darnay's re-arrest in Book II, Chapter 21.

Divide class into small groups of 4-5, depending on class size and number of individuals needed for each scene. Assign each group a scene (or have groups select their own scenes), and explain to the students that they will be reading their assigned/ selected scene as a small group, turning it into a 3-5 minute scripted re-enactment, and performing their scene for the class. Specify that all students should have a speaking or acting role in the performance, but not all lines and passages written in each scene need to be included--it is up to the discretion of the group to include lines and interactions they think are most relevant to conveying the characters and story.

Give groups time to read the passages, prepare their scripts, and assign roles. After writing their scripts, give groups time to practice and prepare for performance.

Finally, have each of the groups perform their scene in front of the class, while others groups watch and complete evaluation slips for the other groups' performances.

Note: Depending on time, this activity can be split into multiple days. Alternatively, students can perform shorter scenes.

Ideas for Differentiated Instruction:

- Assign different roles to different students based on skill areas or areas for growth.
- Give students challenge/analysis questions to analyze about other groups performances.
- Provide some students with additional supports or assistance in preparing for their performance during the prep time (e.g. teacher will spend more time helping some groups brainstorm to devise the best approach).
- Assign different scenes (with different complexities and numbers of challenging vocabulary words) to different groups based on reading level.

Assessment Ideas:

- Students evaluate and notate the dramatic and literary elements in their assigned scene.
- Students perform their scene in front of the class.
- Students complete and submit reflections on or assessments of other groups' performances (qualitative or quantitative).
- After the performances, students can answer questions from others in the class about what choices they made about creating the mood (e.g. how did you decide how certain lines would be read or interpreted?)

Day 4 - Reading Assignment, Questions, Vocabulary

Students read Book II, Chapter 22-Book III, Chapter 7.

Common Core Objectives

- CCSS.ELA-Literacy.CCRA.R.1 Read closely to determine what the text says explicitly and to make logical inferences from it; cite specific textual evidence when writing or speaking to support conclusions drawn from the text.

- CCSS.ELA-Literacy.CCRA.R.2 Determine central ideas or themes of a text and analyze their development; summarize the key supporting details and ideas.

- CCSS.ELA-Literacy.CCRA.R.4 Interpret words and phrases as they are used in a text, including determining technical, connotative, and figurative meanings, and analyze how specific word choices shape meaning or tone.

- CCSS.ELA-Literacy.CCRA.R.6 Assess how point of view or purpose shapes the content and style of a text

- CCSS.ELA-Literacy.CCRA.W.6 Use technology, including the Internet, to produce and publish writing and to interact and collaborate with others.

- CCSS.ELA-Literacy.CCRA.W.7 Conduct short as well as more sustained research projects based on focused questions, demonstrating understanding of the subject under investigation.

- CCSS.ELA-Literacy.CCRA.W.8 Gather relevant information from multiple print and digital sources, assess the credibility and accuracy of each source, and integrate the information while avoiding plagiarism.

- CCSS.ELA-Literacy.CCRA.L.5 Demonstrate understanding of figurative language, word relationships, and nuances in word meanings.

- CCSS.ELA-Literacy.CCRA.SL.4 Present information, findings, and supporting evidence such that listeners can follow the line of reasoning and the organization, development, and style are appropriate to task, purpose, and audience.

Note that it is perfectly fine to expand any day's work into two days depending on the characteristics of the class, particularly if the class will engage in all of the suggested classroom exercises and activities and discuss all of the thought questions.

Content Summary for Teachers

Book II, Chapter 22

A week after the storming of the Bastille, Madame Defarge and the Vengeance are conversing when Monsieur Defarge comes in and tells them that a new aristocrat has been discovered who they must punish. This aristocrat, Foulon, apparently told peasants who were starving to death to eat grass. The Defarges join the mob, which has tied a bundle of grass to Foulon. The mob hangs Foulon from a lamppost and, still thirsty for violence, they then murder Foulon's son-in-law. After these killings, the members of the mob return home, bonded together after their day of killing.

Book II, Chapter 23

Saint Antoine has changed since the overthrow of the aristocrats, as has France more broadly. While the aristocrats and royalty were oppressive, they also provided a sense of social structure, national pride, and symbolic luxury, all of which are now absent.

Two of the Jacques meet in the countryside. One explains to the other that he has been walking for days and must rest, and he asks the latter Jacques, the road-mender, to wake him at the end of the work-day. The road-mender watches Jacques while he sleeps and wakes him when he's done working for the day, and the two men return to town together.

Back in town, a crowd of peasants watches the Monseigneur's château burning down without offering to help put it out. Monsieur Gabelle looks on nervously. The peasant mob then follows Gabelle back to his house shouting at him for being a tax collector. Afraid, Gabelle barricades himself in his house and devises a plan--if the mob attacks, he will jump off his roof in order to crush some of the people in the mob below. The mob continues with their reign of violence, burning down other noblemen's châteaux and killing government officials, but Gabelle is spared.

Book II, Chapter 24

The French Revolution continues for three more years--the monarchy is eliminated completely and the noblemen are being killed off. Tellson's has become a major hub for information about the revolution, as many Frenchmen who are fleeing stop there first when they arrive in London. Charles Darnay visits Mr. Lorry at the bank to try to convince him not to go to Paris on business. Upon hearing Mr. Stryver speaking with men of Monseigneur's class about punishing the peasants after the revolution ends, Darnay is somewhat alarmed.

Darnay also overhears a bank clerk asking Mr. Lorry if he had found Marquis St. Evrémonde, for whom the bank has a letter. The other French noblemen all say that, while they don't know Evrémonde personally, they do know that he supported the revolution and gave his land away to his peasants. Darnay says that he knows Evrémonde and, upon receiving the letter, opens it. The letter is an urgent request for help from Monsieur Gabelle who has now been imprisoned. While Darnay believes he was right to renounce his French title, he also worries that he did not leave everything in proper order, and decides that he must go to France to sort it all out. He presumes and hopes that his abdication of his title will endear him to the French revolutionaries. Darnay tells Mr. Lorry that Marquis St. Evrémonde--whose true identity is Darnay, though Lorry is unaware of this at the time--has received the plea for help and is on his way to Paris. Darnay departs London at night in secret, leaving letters for Lucie and Dr. Manette to explain his sudden departure.

Book III, Chapter 1

The revolution has caused France to become very chaotic and disorganized and, as a result, Darnay's journey there is slow and he is frequently stopped for questioning. As he nears Paris, someone wakes him in the middle of the night to tell him that he must have an escort to enter the city. Monsieur Defarge is Darnay's escort. Upon entering the town of Beauvais, peasants mob Darnay shouting, "down with the emigrant!" Darnay is concerned for his safety. The day Darnay departed from England, a decree was passed saying that the property of emigrants could be sold off and they could be condemned to death upon their return.

Upon his arrival in Paris, Darnay is imprisoned in La Force. Defarge refuses to help Darnay, despite knowing that he is married to Lucie Manette. Darnay is surprised at the politeness and kindness of the other prisoners in La Force. As he sees what prison life is like, however, he begins to understand why Dr. Manette took up shoemaking.

Book III, Chapter 2

At the Tellson's Bank branch in Paris, Mr. Lorry reflects that many French noblemen will not live long enough to get their money from the bank. He hears a rising commotion outside and is thankful that no one close to him is in Paris. At this point, Lucie and Dr. Manette come in and report that Darnay is in prison. Luckily, the revolutionaries leave Manette alone, respectful of the time he spent imprisoned in the Bastille.

After Lucie goes to another room, Mr. Lorry and Dr. Manette observe the angry mob in the courtyard, sharpening their weapons on a grindstone. Mr. Lorry informs Dr. Manette that prisoners in La Force are being murdered. Concerned about Darnay's fate, Dr. Manette rushes down to the courtyard and tells the mob that he was a prisoner in the Bastille. They praise him as a hero and carry him to La Force, now eager to save Darnay because of their respect for Dr. Manette.

Book III, Chapter 3

Concerned about endangering Tellson's bank by continuing to house Lucie--the wife of an emigrant prisoner--there, Mr. Lorry decides to find an apartment for them near his own. Jerry Cruncher now guards the apartment that Lucie, young Lucie, Dr. Manette, and Miss Pross now inhabit.

When Mr. Lorry returns to his home, Monsieur Defarge visits with a message from Dr. Manette, informing Lorry that both Manette and Darnay are safe, but they must remain in prison for the time being. Defarge has a message for Lucie as well, so Lorry accompanies him to her apartment. On their way there, the two men are joined by Madame Defarge. Lucie is thrilled to receive news that her husband is safe and she kisses Madame Defarge's hand in gratitude. Madame Defarge does not respond.

Mr. Lorry tells Lucie that Madame Defarge wants to see everyone in the family so she knows who to protect when protests break out. Lucie asks Madame Defarge to protect her husband, but the latter responds that she has witnessed far too much suffering to care much for the difficulties of one woman.

Book III, Chapter 4

Over the course of four days, 1,100 prisoners are killed in La Force. Luckily for Darnay, Dr. Manette's emphasis on his imprisonment in the Bastille earns both of them protection from the angry mobs. Manette is almost able to get Darnay out immediately, but at the last minute, Darnay is put back in his cell. Dr. Manette stays with Darnay in his cell to make sure he is protected.

Dr. Manette tends to a prisoner who was released but then attacked with a pike. He cares for both the victim and the attacker, and his ability to use his skills again for good gives him a sense purpose. He is glad to be able to use his influence to help Darnay and convey regular messages between Darnay and Lucie.

Despite Dr. Manette's best efforts, he is unable to get Darnay released from prison right away, because the Revolution has moved so fast. Darnay ends up staying in prison for a year and three months.

Book III, Chapter 5

For a year and three months, Lucie remains unsure if her husband is dead or alive. She maintains their new home in Paris and keeps her spirits up by doing little things to make her feel as if Charles is there with her. When Dr. Manette tells Lucie that there is a section of the sidewalk where Darnay may be able to see Lucie at certain hours of the day if she walks past, Lucie faithfully walks back and forth past this area for hours every day.

The fourth Jacques has now become a wood-sawyer and cuts wood near Lucie's daily walking route. He makes fun of her for coming to see someone in prison everyday. In December, a massive crowd that includes Jacques Four and the Vengeance pursue Lucie during her walk. Although she is alarmed, Dr. Manette assures her that no harm will come to her, and Madame Defarge salutes them as she passes. The next day, Darnay is brought to court.

Book III, Chapter 6

Charles Darnay is put on trial with twenty-three other people the next day and he bids farewell to his friends in prison. The next morning at the Tribunal he observes that it seems like criminals are in charge of trying innocents. Darnay is on trial for being an emigrant and his choice to renounce his aristocratic title seems to have no bearing on the court's opinion of him. People cry out for him to be beheaded. Darnay then explains that he is married to Lucie Manette, to which the crowd responds with cheers.

Gabelle and Dr. Manette both testify on Darnay's behalf, noting that, far from sympathizing with the aristocracy, he is a friend to both France and America. Darnay is set free and the crowd praises him. Lucie is overjoyed to see Darnay again in person and she tenderly thanks her father for his help in getting her husband released.

Book III, Chapter 7

Because of the costs associated with Darnay's imprisonment, the household became very meticulous with their finances. Despite scaling back, they are still relatively wealthy compared to many around them, so Jerry Cruncher and Miss Pross had to shop separately to keep others from noticing their wealth. They both pronounce their devotion to the King and England.

After Pross and Cruncher leave, four men arrive at the home and re-arrest Darnay. They claim that he has been accused by the Defarges and another unnamed person.

Thought Questions (students consider while they read)

1. What do you think the significance of the title of Book the Second--"The Golden Thread"--is? How does it relate to characters and broader themes in the novel?

2. What do you think makes Charles Darnay feel that he must return to France? What does this reveal about his character? What themes might he represent in the novel?

3. How does Dickens incorporate his complex views about class, poverty, and social injustice into his clear criticism of the violence employed by the revolutionaries from the end of Book II through the beginning of Book III?

4. How does the scene at the grindstone in Book III, Chapter 2 resemble the scene in Book II, Chapter 5 in which the wine-cask breaks outside the Defarge's wine-shop? What is the significance of these parallels?

5. How do shadows, and the relationship between light and darkness, play out over the course of Book III, Chapters 3-5?

Vocabulary (in order of appearance)

"...in which to soften his modicum of hard and bitter bread to such extent as he could..." (II.22)

modicum:

A small amount or piece.

"...and the winnowing of many bushels of words, Madame Defarge's frequent experessions of impatience were tken up..." (II.22)

winnow:

To blow air through grain to remove the lighter particles (the chaff), often used metaphorically.

"...and otherwise beatified and beatifying features of Monseigneur." (II.23)

beatify:

Bless, canonize, make holy.

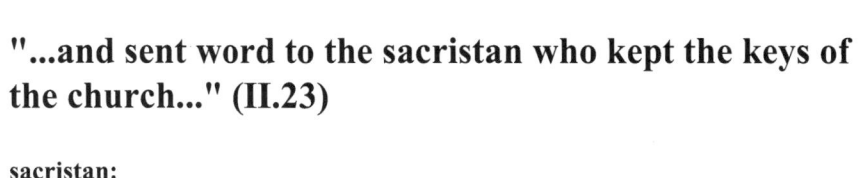

"...and sent word to the sacristan who kept the keys of the church..." (II.23)

sacristan:

A church sexton, one who looks after the sacristy.

"...that there might be need to ring the tocsin by-and-by." (II.23)

tocsin:

An alarm of some kind.

"In the roaring and raging of the conflagration, a red-hot wind, driving straight from the infernal regions..." (II.23)

conflagration:

A huge fire or blaze.

"...trees at a distance, fired by the four fierce figures, begirt he blazing edifice with a new forest of smoke." (II.23)

begirt:

Surround, encompass.

"...Tellson's was a munificent house, and extended great liberality to old customers who had fallen from their high estate." (II.24)

munificent:

Bountiful, generous.

"The penitential den once set apart for interviews with the House, was now the news-Exchange..." (II.24)

penitential:

Related to penance or repentance.

"...was hard to be endured without some remonstrance by any sane mane who knew the truth." (II.24)

remonstrance:

A forceful complaint or protest.

"And it was such vapouring all about his ears, like a troublesome confusion of blood in his own head..." (II.24)

vapouring:

Blustering, boasting (archaic).

"...infected bythe most pestilent and blasphemous code of devilry that ever was known..." (II.24)

pestilent:

Deadly, dangerous.

"...before the sequestration of emigrant property, I have remitted the imposts they had ceased to pay..." (II.24)

sequestration:

The act of legally taking over someone's assets in order to pay debts.

"...Monsieur heretofore the Marquis, to succour and release me." (II.24)

succour:

Help, support, aid.

"'You are a cursed emigrant,' cried a farrier, making at him in a furious manner through the press..." (III.1)

farrier:

A person who makes horseshoes and trims their hooves.

"...and by the sudden emergence from ambuscase, and sharp reining up across their way..." (III.1)

ambuscade:

An ambush or sudden attack.

"'Tut, tut!' said Mr. Lorry; 'what is this despondency in the brave little breast?...'" (III.3)

despondency:

Despair, hopelessness.

"...still, the sagacious Mr. Lorry saw that there was a new sustaining pride in it." (III.4)

sagacious:

Clever, wise, knowledgeable.

"...the delicate foot mincing in this slough of blood and dirt, were types of the disjointed time." (III.5)

slough:

Deep mire or mod, like a swamp.

"...and Jerry (almost wholly transferred to them by Mr. Lorry) ad become their daily retainer..." (III.7)

retainer:

Something that holds something else in place or together.

Additional Homework

1. As an extension of today's Character Sketches classroom activity, write 2-3 paragraphs explaining the character representation you created earlier and and how it represents your selected character.

2. Find an extended reference to Charles Dickens or his plays in popular culture--a musical piece, a movie, a TV show, a book, an exhibit, anything you choose--and bring the example in to share in class.

Day 4 - Discussion of Thought Questions

1. What do you think the significance of the title of Book the Second--"The Golden Thread"--is? How does it relate to characters and broader themes in the novel?

Time:

7-10 minutes

Discussion:

In Book the Second, we see Lucie and her father build their relationship after numerous years apart, several different men fall in love with her, her marriage to Darnay and the beginning of their own family. In short, many important plot developments take place over the course of this Book and Lucie is directly or indirectly connected to virtually all of them.

On a purely literal level, Lucie's golden blonde hair is emblematic of her magnetic beauty that attracts virtually every many she meets. Dickens uses her golden hair, however, to symbolize the goodness of her heart and how she binds her family together. He refers to her as "the golden thread" that keeps the family going. It is Lucie who connects Sydney Carton to Charles Darnay, Darnay to Doctor Manette, and Mr. Lorry to the family more broadly, and she is the motivation for many of the men in the story to pursue a greater purpose in their lives. Indeed, many of the characters give at least a passing thought to Lucie Manette's golden hair, suggesting that it has a symbolic power for many. For example, Jacques Three thinks about how much he'd like to see Lucie's golden hair on the guillotine's chopping block. Yet this will never come to pass, of course, as her hair also serves as something like a good luck charm for her and connects her to those she loves throughout the novel.

2. What do you think makes Charles Darnay feel that he must return to France? What does this reveal about his character?

What themes might he represent in the novel?

Time:

7-10 minutes

Discussion:

As a reminder, at the end of Book II, Darnay overhears a bank clerk at Tellson's Bank asking Mr. Lorry if he had found Marquis St. Evrémonde, for whom the bank has a letter. The other French noblemen all say that, while they don't know Evrémonde personally, they do know that he supported the revolution and gave his land away to his peasants. Darnay says that he knows Evrémonde and, upon receiving the letter, opens it. The letter is an urgent request for help from Monsieur Gabelle who has now been imprisoned. While Darnay believes he was right to renounce his French title, he also worries that he did not leave everything in proper order, and decides that he must go to France to sort it all out. He presumes and hopes that his abdication of his title will endear him to the French revolutionaries. Darnay tells Mr. Lorry that Marquis St. Evrémonde--whose true identity is Darnay, though Lorry is unaware of this at the time--has received the plea for help and is on his way to Paris. Darnay departs London at night in secret, leaving letters for Lucie and Dr. Manette to explain his sudden departure.

Darnay's decision to go back to France, despite the risks there because of his social class, reveals a lot about his character. Namely, this decision reflects Darnay's admirable goodness and virtue, but also suggests that he may be a bit overly-optimistic and naïve about the likelihood of a positive result coming out of his return to a land suffering such extreme upheaval and chaos. This is a yet another example of a frequent issue that has bothered many readers and critics over the years regarding Darnay's character (and, in fact, Lucie Manette's character as well): they are both somewhat boring and one-dimensional, and neither of them grows or changes much over the course of the novel. Despite this seeming lack of depth, Darnay and Lucie both serve two important roles in the novel. First, their unyielding commitment to goodness, morality, and justice serves as a stark contrast to Madame Defarge's devotion to vengeful and retaliatory violence. Second, Darnay and Manette's continually manifested kindness and virtue inspires Sydney Carton to believe in a better future for himself and the possibility that he can become a better man.

Moreover, Darnay's sense that **must** return to Paris, as if drawn by a magnet, is a prime example of the theme of Fate & The Passage of Time in *A Tale of Two Cities*. Indeed, many of the characters in the novel feel this sense of the inevitability of Fate, Time, and Destiny like an undertow in their lives: Lucie's interpretation of the noise she keeps hearing of feet echoing through the halls as suggesting that sometime in the future, the past would come back to haunt them; Darnay's sense that he must return to France, despite knowing the dangers there; Carton's sense that he must redeem himself by making significant sacrifices in the future--all of these continually draw upon the sense of inevitability associated with a Fate-driven universe. Expanding this idea even more broadly, throughout the novel, Fate is portrayed with a portentous tone rather than positive one. This dark over-arching tone is especially notable in Dickens's portrayal of Madame Defarge as resembling one of the Fates of classical tragic myth, which served to connect the future its ultimate dark ending.

3. How does Dickens incorporate his complex views about class, poverty, and social injustice into his clear criticism of the violence employed by the revolutionaries from the end of Book II through the beginning of Book III?

Time:

7-10 minutes

Discussion:

For Dickens, the French Revolution brought up many challenging issues, as he was a staunch political progressive himself who advocated for radical reforms of poor laws of the era and significant changes to England's approach to social inequity. *A Tale of Two Cities* demonstrates Dickens's conflicting feelings about the Revolution. He writes in great depth and detail about the poverty and oppression the French peasants suffered and vividly illustrates the callous barbarity of the aristocracy, suggesting that he understands the revolutionaries' motivations. Many of the most egregious examples of the abuses by the aristocracy come earlier in Book II and later in Book III, but students may call upon these examples from the novel, as well as primary source examples from their research in the Researching the Revolution activity from Day #3.

At the same time, Dickens also unsparingly portrays the brutality of the revolutionaries' methods as they gain power and influence. Dickens clearly believes that there was significant justification for the peasants' desire for a societal overthrown. Ultimately however, despite his personal sympathies, Dickens sides with the argument against the Revolution, because of the overkill and bloodthirstiness of the revolutionaries as the movement gains more power. The novel also shows this transformation over the course of the story, demonstrating the evolution of the revolutionary movement from its focus on social justice and equality to a focus on retribution and revenge.

Related to the novel's focus on Class Struggle, the theme of Inversions & Reversal, an inevitable result of a story surrounding a sociological event like the French Revolution, is also a significant part of these chapters of the novel. This Revolution completely mixed up French society and turned all of the societal norms on their heads. For example, upon his return to France, Darnay notes that in the new social order, noblemen are in prison with outlaws as their judges, juries, and executioners.

4. How does the scene at the grindstone in Book III, Chapter 2 resemble the scene in Book II, Chapter 5 in which the wine-cask breaks outside the Defarge's wine-shop? What is the significance of these parallels?

Time:

7-10 minutes

Discussion:

In Book II, Chapter 2, Mr. Lorry and Dr. Manette observe the angry mob in the courtyard, sharpening their weapons on a grindstone. Mr. Lorry informs Dr. Manette that prisoners in La Force are being murdered. Concerned about Darnay's fate, Dr. Manette rushes down to the courtyard and tells the mob that he was a prisoner in the Bastille. They praise him as a hero and carry him to La Force, now eager to save Darnay because of their respect for Dr. Manette.

Dickens's language and imagery in this scene at the grindstone--including lines like "[not one] creature in the group free from the smear of blood" (261)--immediately reminds the reader of the scene in Book II, Chapter 5 in which the wine-cask breaks outside the Defarge's wine-shop and the starving peasants rush to lap it up. These scenes serve as parallels of each other and demonstrate Dickens's artistry with language and powerful skill with evocative imagery. Early on, Dickens linked the symbolism of the broken cask to blood, and now that imagery has come to its full fruition.

Moreover, the language Dickens uses to describe the revolutionary mob sharpening their weapons reflects the wild, bloodthirsty, and ruthlessly violent tendencies of the revolutionaries as the movement has progressed. The reader senses the continuity and fulfillment of foreshadowing in the way the peasants sharpen their weapons and their faces are smeared with blood, just as they were smeared with wine early in Book II. This over-arching theme is even more thoroughly reinforced by the frequent recurrence of circle-like shapes and symbols to suggest the cyclical nature of time, fate, and human nature.

5. How do shadows, and the relationship between light and darkness, play out over the course of Book III, Chapters 3-5?

Time:

7-10 minutes

Discussion:

Although shadows appear regularly throughout the novel, "The Shadow" appears as the sub-title of Book II, Chapter 3, suggesting that this imagery will take on particular significance in this chapter. Indeed, Dickens emphasizes the contrast between darkness and light occurs from the very beginning of the novel, beginning with the eerie, precarious journey of the mail-coach that Mr. Lorry rides to Dover. One of the brightest spots in the novel comes on the happy day of Lucie's wedding in Book II, Chapter 18. However, by this point, Dickens's focus on duality in the novel means that there must be an impending shadow must inevitably fall over the happy, charmed life of Charles Darnay and Lucie Manette. Madame Defarge casts that looming, foreboding shadow on their lives in these chapters.

In Chapter 3, Dickens describes "the shadow attendant on Madame Defarge and her party" as seeming to fall "so threatening and dark on the child, that her mother instinctively kneeled on the ground beside her" (266). After Lucie kneels down protectively over her daughter, "the shadow attendant on Madame Defarge and her party seemed then to fall, threatening and dark, on both the mother and the child" (266). Madame Defarge's looming, dark presence, and Lucie's apparent fear and alarm at her presence foreshadows the battle between light and dark that will be playing out over the chapters to come.

Day 4 - Short Answer Evaluation

1. What is the name of the revolutionary group that the Defarges are a part of?

   _____

2. Who is Monsieur Gabelle?

   _____

3. What is the true identity of Marquis St. Evrémonde?

   _____

4. Where is Darnay imprisoned when he arrives in Paris?

   _____

5. Why does the angry mob praise and celebrate Dr. Manette?

   _____

6. For how long does Darnay stay in prison?

   _____

7. Who walks by Darnay's window in his prison cell on a near-daily basis, hoping to see him?

   _____

8. What profession does the fourth Jacques take up?

   _____

9. What is Darnay put on trial for?

_____

10. Why is Darnay re-arrested?

_____

Answer Key

1. The Vengeance.
2. He is a tax collector in Saint Antoine.
3. Charles Darnay.
4. La Force.
5. He tells the mob that he was a prisoner in the Bastille.
6. One year and three months.
7. His wife, Lucie.
8. He becomes a wood-sawyer.
9. He is put on trial for being an emigrant.
10. He has been accused by the Defarges and another unnamed person.

Day 4 - Crossword Puzzle

ACROSS

1. Huge fire or blaze.
3. Darnay is imprisoned in __ _____
7. Where Dr. Manette was imprisoned.
8. Clever, wise, knowledgeable.
10. An alarm of some kind.
11. Deadly, dangerous.
12. The Defarges revolutionary group. The
   _____.
16. Jacques becomes a ____-_____
18. Help, support, aid.
19. Revolutionaries' execution method of choice.
20. Darnay's former surname.

DOWN

2. Monsieur _____ is a tax collector.
4. Forceful complaint or protest.
5. Bountiful, generous.
6. Despair, hopelessness.
9. Who is out to get Darnay?
13. The 2nd time, Darnay is arrested for being an
   _____.
14. A small amount or piece.
15. Bless, canonize, make holy.
17. Who walks by Darnay's cell daily?

Crossword Puzzle Answer Key

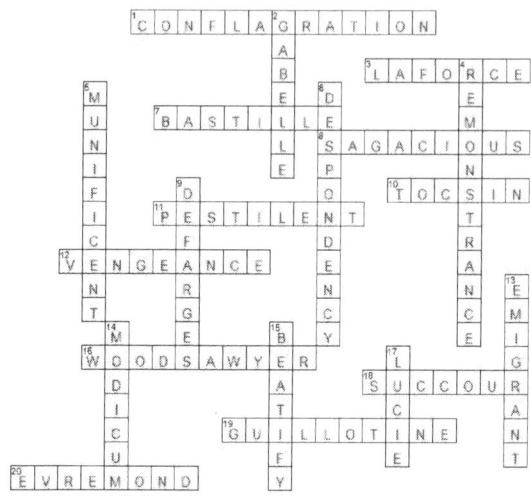

ACROSS
1. Huge fire or blaze.
3. Darnay is imprisoned in __ _____
7. Where Dr. Manette was imprisoned.
8. Clever, wise, knowledgeable.
10. An alarm of some kind.
11. Deadly, dangerous.
12. The Defarges revolutionary group: The
   _____
16. Jacques becomes a ____-____
18. Help, support, aid.
19. Revolutionaries' execution method of choice.
20. Darnay's former surname.

DOWN
2. Monsieur _____ is a tax collector.
4. Forceful complaint or protest.
5. Bountiful, generous.
6. Despair, hopelessness.
9. Who is out to get Darnay?
13. The 2nd time, Darnay is arrested for being an
   _____
14. A small amount or piece.
15. Bless, canonize, make holy.
17. Who walks by Darnay's cell daily?

Day 4 - Vocabulary Quiz

Terms

1. _____ modicum
2. _____ beatify
3. _____ tocsin
4. _____ conflagration
5. _____ begirt
6. _____ munificent
7. _____ pestilent
8. _____ succour
9. _____ despondency
10. _____ sagacious

Answers

A. A huge fire or blaze.
B. Bless, canonize, make holy.
C. An alarm of some kind.
D. Bountiful, generous.
E. Despair, hopelessness.
F. Deadly, dangerous.
G. Help, support, aid.
H. A small amount or piece.
I. Clever, wise, knowledgeable.
J. Surround, encompass.

Answer Key

1. H modicum: A small amount or piece.
2. B beatify: Bless, canonize, make holy.
3. C tocsin: An alarm of some kind.
4. A conflagration: A huge fire or blaze.
5. J begirt: Surround, encompass.
6. D munificent: Bountiful, generous.
7. F pestilent: Deadly, dangerous.
8. G succour: Help, support, aid.
9. E despondency: Despair, hopelessness.
10. I sagacious: Clever, wise, knowledgeable.

Day 4 - Classroom Activities

1. The Life and Times of Charles Dickens

Kind of Activity:

Long-term Project

Objective:

Students will conduct research on life in late 18th and early 19th century England, examine how specific societal changes may have impacted Dickens's life and writings, and present their research and findings to the class.

Common Core Standards:

CCSS.ELA-Literacy.CCRA.R.4, CCSS.ELA-Literacy.CCRA.R.5, CCSS.ELA-Literacy.CCRA.SL.4

Time:

20-25 minutes (recurring)

Structure:

For an overview of this unit-long project, see the description in Day #1.

For Day #4, review the purpose of the activity and how it will continue through the unit. Then, demonstrate how to find important details from researching the world events and societal developments in England happening during Dickens's lifetime that could have impacted his perspectives about particular important themes in his writing. For example, identify the French Revolution and the rule of Queen Victoria as a significant cultural shift in England that impacted Dickens's and others' worldviews. Then identify a textual example of this theme arising in the Day #4 readings. Next, check for understanding, asking students questions about the observations and inferences made about the selected theme. Then, depending on student understanding, lead students in a guided practice--identifying another event or aspect of Dickens's life and a textual example of a related theme--or proceed to splitting students into groups.

As in previous days of this activity, have the pre-assigned each group continue to research their assigned or selected theme. As mentioned previously, themes might include: Science & Technology; Rebellions/Revolutions in the late 18th and early 19th centuries; Queen Victoria's reign; Dickens's Religious Worldview/Outlook, Dickens's Literary & Philosophical influences; Literature in the Victorian era, Cultural/Religious Reactions to the French Revolution, etc.

Provide biographical sources on Dickens for students to read independently, or have them begin conducting their own research, depending on the time and resources available. These resources could include any of the following, in addition to many others:

Victorian England:

- http://www.english.uwosh.edu/roth/VictorianEngland.htm
- http://www.bbc.co.uk/history/british/victorians/
- http://www.aboutbritain.com/articles/victorian-era-1837-1901.asp
- https://www.wwnorton.com/college/english/nael/victorian/review/summary.htm
- http://www.history.ac.uk/ihr/Focus/Victorians/article.html
- https://www.history.org.uk/resources/primary_resource_3871_134.html

Charles Dickens:

- http://www.biography.com/people/charles-dickens-9274087
- http://www.bbc.co.uk/history/historic_figures/dickens_charles.shtml
- http://www.online-literature.com/dickens/
- http://www.britannica.com/biography/Charles-Dickens-British-novelist
- http://www.dickens-online.info/charles-dickens-biography.htm
- http://www.pbs.org/wgbh/masterpiece/dickens/dickens.html
- http://charlesdickenspage.com/
- http://dickensmuseum.com/
- http://dickenslive.com/
- http://www.dickensfellowship.org/life-charles-dickens

A Tale of Two Cities Analysis:

- http://www.gradesaver.com/tale-of-two-cities
- http://www.novelguide.com/a-tale-of-two-cities/theme-analysis
- http://www.litcharts.com/lit/a-tale-of-two-cities/plot-overview
- http://www.online-literature.com/dickens/twocities/
- http://charlesdickenspage.com/cities.html
- http://www.pbs.org/wgbh/masterpiece/archive/110/110.html

As in Days #1-3, the group scribe should chart the sociological events related to their group's theme, with a particular eye toward the ways that Day #4's readings have expanded their understanding of their assigned theme. Next, each group will examine the day's readings to find textual examples of the assigned theme. The group will then analyze their selected pieces of textual evidence and add them to their overall analysis.

Finally, as in previous days, students will then share out one finding from their group with the whole class.

Ideas for Differentiated Instruction:

- Give students reading sections for research differentiated by reading level.
- Provide some groups with the option to read aloud the biographical section, or listen to/watch audio or video pieces about Dickens as a form of research.
- Assign students different roles—scribe, head researcher, lead note-taker, presenter, etc.—based on skills or areas for growth.
- Split students into groups by skill-set or areas of need, so that some groups can work more independently, and the teacher can support other groups more as needed.

Assessment Ideas:

- Student groups each generate a series of charts about an aspect of life or culture in Dickens's time and how it relates to his writings, with specific references to scenes from *A Tale of Two Cities*.
- Students present findings from group chart to the rest of the class.
- Students take notes, using an interactive handout (digital or paper), on other groups' theme presentations.
- Students present overall research and analysis at end of unit, using multimedia (audio/video/picture) presentations.

2. Creatively Representating the Characters from A Tale of Two Cities

Kind of Activity:

Artistic Response

Objective:

Students will analyze and evaluate the representations of one of the characters in the novel, select a means of creatively representing the character's personality, and demonstrate their creative representation to the class.

Common Core Standards:

CCSS.ELA-Literacy.CCRA.W.6, CCSS.ELA-Literacy.CCRA.SL.5

Time:

40-45 minutes

Structure:

Throughout his representations of the various characters in *A Tale of Two Cities*, Dickens uses extensive imagery and evocative metaphors to demonstrate the vast differences in the different characters' personalities and their different approaches to the French revolution and other cultural and societal shifts of the time. In this activity, students will construct a creative representation of one of character's personalities, as represented by Dickens, in whatever way they choose.

There can be limitations on the types of media students are allowed to employ, or they can have free reign (e.g. dramatization or performance, painting, drawing, musical response, mural, audio-visual interpretation, etc.). In addition, this project can be done in small groups or individually.

Explain the overall premise of the activity to students, giving an example of how one might choose to artistically represent an aspect of one of the characters from *A Tale of Two Cities*. Depending on how the activity is constructed--with limitless creative license or specific options, being done in small groups or individually--explain the structure, rules, and limitations of the activity to students. Students can use the charts created about the different characters during the Day #2 activity reflecting on the reading and the PBS mini-series, as well as any other resources you want to make available for research. Make sure to note how long students will have to complete the project, what creative materials and resources are available to them, and, if the project is being done in groups, how roles should be assigned.

Give students the remainder of the time to construct or complete their projects. Note: this activity could be extended over multiple class sessions or given as a take-home assignment.

Once the students' creative responses are complete, have students present their artistic representations to the class.

Ideas for Differentiated Instruction:

- Depending on student independence, assign them to work as individuals or in small groups.

- Split students into groups by skill-set or areas of need, so that some groups can work more independently, and the teacher can support other groups more (e.g. participating in the student discussion, helping to make connections, etc.).
- Assign different students or groups different sister's personalities to interpret, based on the poems' levels of complexity.

Assessment Ideas:

- Students present or perform their artistic representation to the class and are graded (by the teacher) based on a rubric.
- Students offer feedback on other students' artistic representations, either in verbal or written form.
- Students write a 1-2 paragraph response about the artistic process of creating their piece.

3. Surprise Scene Workshop, Part I: Writing Your Own "A Tale of Two Cities" Scene

Kind of Activity:

Creative Writing

Objective:

Students will be able to understand Dickens's use of imagery and symbols to convey larger themes, write their own scene using selected symbols and themes, and explain their use of symbolism to the class during a scene reading or performance.

Common Core Standards:

CCSS.ELA-Literacy.CCRA.R.3, CCSS.ELA-Literacy.CCRA.W.3

Time:

40-45 minutes

Structure:

In this activity, students will have to write an additional "bonus" scene for *A Tale of Two Cities*, using randomly selected themes and symbols (one of each, and based on those used by Dickens). To introduce the activity, explain the way in which Dickens often uses unique symbols and imagery to discuss and explain much larger societal and existential concepts. Explain that, now that the class is more familiar with Dickens's style and the overall plot and characters in *A Tale of Two Cities*, they are going to write their own creative scenes using Dickens's symbolism, imagery, and thematic styles themselves.

Show how students will participate in this activity by randomly selecting a theme and a symbol (both related to Dickens's *A Tale of Two Cities*), brainstorming briefly about how to correlate the theme to the symbol. Then demonstrate writing the first paragraph or so of a scene. Make sure to note for students that, while the symbol they select should play a primary role in their scene, it does not have to be the only symbol they use and can be incorporated into a larger extended metaphor--this will give students more flexibility and options for expressing themselves, while keeping the complexity of instructions to a minimum. In addition, tell students that their scene must be at least 2 pages (no maximum), must include at least 2 characters from the novel, and does not necessarily need to be written with the structure and form of Dickens's style.

Next, have students pick one theme and one symbol at random (e.g. write them on slips of paper in two separate bowls and have students pick them, or hand cards out to students randomly). Then, have the class get to writing.

After students have finished writing, have students read their scenes to a partner or small group and explain how they chose to combine their symbol and theme in writing the scene. Alternatively, ask 1-2 students to share their scenes aloud and explain their creative choices to the class as a whole.

Ideas for Differentiated Instruction:

- Select specific students to read their scenes aloud, based on reading level and comfort with public reading.
- Provide some students with sentence starters or leading questions to help them understand and interpret their selected theme and symbol.
- This activity could also be done in small groups to facilitate different students' skills and writing abilities. In addition, this writing project could be continued as an at-home project if students are unable to finish it in the time allotted.

Assessment Ideas:

- Give students the opportunity to provide feedback on their peers' scenes and fill out an evaluation rubric.
- Have students turn in their scenes for teacher assessment or editing.
- Ask students to write 1-2 paragraphs reflecting on the process of writing the scene, and why they chose to combine their selected symbol and theme as they did.

Day 5 - Reading Assignment, Questions, Vocabulary

Students read Book III, Chapters 8-15.

Common Core Objectives

- CCSS.ELA-Literacy.CCRA.R.1 Read closely to determine what the text says explicitly and to make logical inferences from it; cite specific textual evidence when writing or speaking to support conclusions drawn from the text.

- CCSS.ELA-Literacy.CCRA.R.2 Determine central ideas or themes of a text and analyze their development; summarize the key supporting details and ideas.

- CCSS.ELA-Literacy.CCRA.R.4 Interpret words and phrases as they are used in a text, including determining technical, connotative, and figurative meanings, and analyze how specific word choices shape meaning or tone.

- CCSS.ELA-Literacy.CCRA.R.6 Assess how point of view or purpose shapes the content and style of a text

- CCSS.ELA-Literacy.CCRA.W.6 Use technology, including the Internet, to produce and publish writing and to interact and collaborate with others.

- CCSS.ELA-Literacy.CCRA.W.7 Conduct short as well as more sustained research projects based on focused questions, demonstrating understanding of the subject under investigation.

- CCSS.ELA-Literacy.CCRA.W.8 Gather relevant information from multiple print and digital sources, assess the credibility and accuracy of each source, and integrate the information while avoiding plagiarism.

- CCSS.ELA-Literacy.CCRA.L.5 Demonstrate understanding of figurative language, word relationships, and nuances in word meanings.

- CCSS.ELA-Literacy.CCRA.SL.4 Present information, findings, and supporting evidence such that listeners can follow the line of reasoning and the organization, development, and style are appropriate to task, purpose, and audience.

Note that it is perfectly fine to expand any day's work into two days depending on the characteristics of the class, particularly if the class will engage in all of the suggested classroom exercises and activities and discuss all of the thought questions.

Content Summary for Teachers

Book III, Chapter 8

Not knowing of Darnay's re-arrest, Miss Pross and Jerry Cruncher continue shopping. They visit the Defarges' store to buy wine. Pross screams when she sees her brother, Solomon Pross, in the shop as well. Cruncher is also shocked, because he recognizes the man as the English spy, John Barsad. Although Cruncher is initially unable to come up with the man's name, Sydney Carton arrives and tells him the name.

Carton speaks with Barsad alone and asks him to accompany him to Tellson's Bank. When they arrive, Mr. Lorry also recognizes Barsad as a witness from Darnay's trial. Carton tries to pressure Barsad into helping Darnay, by threatening to reveal his true identity to the French government. He also threatens to reveal Barsad's relationship with Roger Cly. Barsad says that Cly is dead, but Cruncher steps in to say that he checked Cly's coffin and there was no one inside. Barsad finally agrees to help Carton with Darnay's case.

Book III, Chapter 9

Mr. Lorry presses Mr. Cruncher about why he knows Roger Cly was not in the coffin. Cruncher explains that he has to make ends meet somehow, hinting at his unsavory secret profession. When Barsad leaves, Carton tells the others that he could only get a promise to see Darnay before he died. Lorry is surprised by Carton's sympathy and understanding. Lorry is no longer obligated to stay in Paris at this point. Carton earnestly wonders aloud to Lorry if he thinks he has wasted his life, and he expresses envy that the old Mr. Lorry will have friends and family there when he dies.

Carton leaves and goes over to La Force. The wood-sawyer Jacques tells him that he should watch people being guillotined if he had never witnessed it before. Carton is taken aback by this suggestion and, instead, goes to find a chemist's shop. Remembering a prayer from his childhood, he helps a child cross the street. He spends the whole night walking around the city and goes, in the morning, to the courthouse to see Darnay's trial.

In the trial, the tribunal tells the court that Monsieur and Madame Defarge and, shockingly, Dr. Manette are the three people who denounced Darnay. Though Manette objects that this is impossible, Monsieur Defarge brings out the hidden document taken from Dr. Manette's Bastille cell.

Book III, Chapter 10

The document written by Dr. Manette is from 1767, while he was locked away in the Bastille and hidden in the chimney in his cell, and it tells the story of why he was imprisoned. As a young doctor, he was forcibly taken into a carriage by a set of armed twins.

In the document Manette wrote, the carriage drives to a remote house where he finds a beautiful young woman screaming and writhing on a bed, sick with a brain fever. She counts to twelve over and over again and repeats, "my husband, my father, and my brother!" The young woman's brother is also in the house, dying of a knife wound. He tells Manette that the nobleman governing the estate had tried to rape his sister (the first patient), claiming he had a right to do so. As an honorable woman, she resisted, and the lord retaliated by tying her husband to a horse-cart and dragging him until he was dead. As he was dying in his wife's arms, he cried out at every toll of the clock as it struck noon, hence her obsession with the number twelve. The lord then carried off the young woman to rape her and, after moving his other sister to a safe place, the brother went after him, incurring the stab wound, which would soon kill him.

Dr. Manette is alarmed by the whole series of events, especially when he realizes the young woman has very recently become pregnant. The noblemen who initially took Dr. Manette from the street ask him to keep quiet about the whole affair, and are then troubled when he will not accept their payment to him. The noblemen are also unmoved by the young woman's death and take Dr. Manette back to his house. Although he is aware that his story will likely have little impact, he writes a letter to the Minister. The wife of the Marquis St. Evrémonde--the lord who raped the young woman--stops by and wants Dr. Manette's help to make amends for her husband's awful actions. Unfortunately, neither the Marquess nor Manette know where to find the surviving sister. She leaves with her son, Charles Darnay, reflecting that he will bear the brunt of his father's sins if she cannot make amends. Later that night, a man barges into Dr. Manette's residence, burns his letter to the Minister, and gets him thrown into the Bastille. Manette curses the whole family.

After hearing the story, the crowd in the courtroom are in an uproar. The jury sentences Darnay to death in the next twenty-four hours.

Book III, Chapter 11

After the verdict is announced, Lucie hugs Darnay, worrying that it will be the last time she will ever see him. Dr. Manette tries to apologize to them, but Darnay stops him, who reiterates his own feelings of guilt for what his family did to Manette and many others. As Darnay is taken away by guards, Lucie is overcome with emotion and blacks out. Carton carries her out, asking for her not to be revived for the time being, so she will not have to experience as much emotional distress. Before he leaves, Carton whispers, "A life you love," in her ear and kisses her. Hoping for a miracle, Dr. Manette goes out to try to use his influence to save Darnay. Everyone thinks that the situation is hopeless.

Book III, Chapter 12

Mr. Carton goes to the Defarges' wine-shop to have a drink. He overhears the Defarges talking about the Darnay case, and learns that Madame Defarge is actually that younger sister from Dr. Manette's story--the one who was whisked away by her brother to keep her safe--and so has an understandable personal grudge against the Evrémonde family. Carton also learns that Madame Defarge believes the revolution must eliminate all the aristocracy and their associates, while her husband believes in a more moderate approach.

When Carton meets up with Mr. Lorry and Dr. Manette again, he notices that Manette is starting to ask for his shoemaking tools again. Carton asks Lorry to do what he says without asking any questions, and Lorry agrees. In Dr. Manette's coat pocket, Carton finds a certificate allowing him to leave the city. Carton reveals what he learned at the Defarges' wine-shop to Lorry and Manette, explaining that Madame Defarge plans to have the whole family arrested by getting the wood-sawyer to testify against them. He tells Mr. Lorry to get Lucie and her daughter out of the city as soon as possible the next day--they will leave as soon as Carton returns to join them in the carriage. Carton leaves the house, but stops briefly to say farewell to Lucie's window.

Book III, Chapter 13

A crowd of men and women from various backgrounds await execution at the Conciergerie, Charles Darnay among them. He tries to accept that he is going to die. He writes a note to Lucie, apologizing for keeping his true identity a secret and explaining that he had no idea that his family had been connected to her father's imprisonment until the reading of the document in court. Darnay also writes letters to Dr. Manette and Mr. Lorry.

Barsad lets Carton into the prison. Carton persuades Darnay to switch clothes with him and has him take a sleep-inducing sedative. Barsad comes in to take who he believes to be Carton out of the cell--in fact, Carton has stayed behind in Darnay's place and Darnay is now free. A jailer takes Carton to another room to await his execution. A woman there recognizes that he is not Darnay, but does not turn him in and instead asks to hold his "brave hand" as they are taken to the guillotine.

The coach carrying Dr. Manette, Lucie, young Lucie, Mr. Lorry, and sedated Charles Darnay (still disguised as Carton) safely leaves Paris. A man stops them and they are momentarily afraid they've been found out. However, the man just wishes to know how many were put to death that day. When they tell him it was fifty-two, he says that he loves the guillotine.

Book III, Chapter 14

As the fifty-two people await their execution, Madame Defarge, The Vengeance, and the third Jacques hold a meeting in the wood-sawyers hut. Defarge disparages her husband for taking pity for Dr. Manette and his family; she believes every one of them should be executed. She asks the wood-sawyer to testify against the family, saying they were secretly colluding with prisoners. Madame Defarge goes to visit Lucie, who she hopes will be so distressed by her husband's execution that she will speak badly of the Republic, which would give Madame Defarge additional evidence against the family.

When Defarge arrives at the apartment--a pistol and a dagger in hand--she finds only Mr. Cruncher and Miss Pross, who are both alarmed by the day's events and are about to leave the city themselves. When Defarge arrives, Cruncher has just left to prepare the horses for their departure, so only Miss Pross is there. Defarge and Pross get into a heated and eventually physical argument, and Pross accidentally kills Defarge with her own gun. Pross is also permanently deafened by the gun's loud noise. She runs out of the apartment in alarm and she and Cruncher escape Paris on horseback.

Book III, Chapter 15

Much of the final chapter includes philosophical thoughts about the nature of revolution, time, and the future. On the way to the guillotine, Carton stoically ignores everyone except the young woman whose hand he holds to support her. The Vengeance tries to find Madame Defarge at the guillotine, but cannot locate her. Carton continues to hold the girl's hand and she thanks him for his moral support.

Carton goes to his execution peacefully. He prophetically envisions all that will happen in the future to those he knows: Barsad, Cly, Defarge, the Vengeance, the Jury, and the Judge will all eventually be killed by the guillotine and the surrounding blood-thirsty culture they helped create; and Lucie and Darnay will live happily back in England, with all their future generations, including a son named after Carton himself, blessing his goodness and self-sacrifice. As he dies, he concludes, "It is a far, far better thing that I do than I have ever done; it is a far, far better rest than I go to than I have ever known."

Thought Questions (students consider while they read)

1. What do the reader learn about Madame Defarge's background in Book III, Chapters 10 and 12? What does this information and her subsequent actions reveal about her character?

2. What does Madame Defarge's death reveal about her character? And what does it foreshadow for the broader Revolution in France?

3. What is the thematic importance of Sydney Carton's ultimate sacrifice at the end of the novel? How does this event relate to prior instances of this theme (or these themes) earlier in the novel?

4. What do you think of the way that Dickens conveys the importance of family in the novel overall, and especially in Book III? How does this relate to events in his own life at the time?

5. Having now read the end of the novel, what do you think of Carton's character development over the course of the novel? How does he change both his beliefs and actions as the novel proceeds? Why?

Vocabulary (in order of appearance)

"...Miss Pross resorted to The Good Republican Brutus of Antiquity, attended by her cavalier." (III.8)

cavalier:

A small dog with medium-long, silky fur.

"Mr. Lorry immediately remembered, and regarded his new visitor with an undisguised look of abhorrence." (III.8)

abhorrence:

Loathing, disgust.

"'I play my Ace, Denunciation of Mr. Barsad to the nearst Section Commitee.'" (III.8)

denunciation:

Publicly condemning or informing against someone.

"...our English reasons for vaunting our superiority to secrecy and spies are of very modern date..." (III.8)

vaunting:

Bragging, boasting.

"...received such a check from the inscrutability of Carton,--who was a mystery to wiser and honester men than he..." (III.8)

inscrutability:

Hard to understand, mysterious.

"...that Cly was so ferreted up and down, that he never would have got away at all but for that sham." (III.8)

ferret:

To hunt about, search around.

"Mr. Lorry's countenance fell." (III.9)

countenance:

Someone's expression or face.

"'But go and see that droll dog,' the little man persisted..." (III.9)

droll:

Amusing, strangely funny.

"...for the popular revulsion had even travelled the length of self-destruction from years of priestly imposters, plunderers, and profligates..." (III.9)

profligate:

A degenerate or debaucherous person.

"WhenI was clear of the house, a black muffler was drawn tightly over my mouth from behind, and my arms pinioned." (III.10)

pinion:

To hold or tie someone's limbs.

"...he stopped at a shop-window where there was a mirror, and slightly altered and disordered arrangement of his loose cravat, and his coat-collar, and his wild hair." (III.12)

cravat:

A necktie.

"...Madame Defarge cast a casreless glance at him, and then a keener, and then a keener, and then advanced to him herself..." (III.12)

keener:

Someone who leans in or is anxious to hear something.

"...and this woman (the inveteracy of whose pursuit cannot be described) would wait to add that strength to her case..." (III.12)

inveteracy:

Persistence, obstinacy.

"...Madame Defarge held darkly ominous council with The Vengeance and Jacques Three of the Revolutionry Jury." (III.14)

ominous:

Menacing, foreboding.

"'There is no better,' the voluble Vengeance protested in her shrill notes, 'in France.'" (III.14)

voluble:

Wordy, verbose, talkative.

"'And before the tumbrils arrive. Be sure you are there, my soul...'" (III.14)

tumbril:

An open-topped cart that tips to dispense its cargo.

"'I have no doublt it is best that Mrs. Cruncher should have it entirely under her on superintendence.'" (III.14)

superintendence:

Under direction or oversight.

"This was Mr. Cruncher's conclusion after a protracted but vain endeavour to find a better one." (III.14)

protracted:

Long and drawn out, prolonged.

"This exordium, and Miss Pross's two hands in quite agonised entreaty clasping his..." (III.14)

exordium:

Introduction, beginning.

"Sow the same seed of rpacious licence and oppression over again..." (III.15)

rapacious:

Aggressively avaricious or greedy.

Additional Homework

1. As a continuation of today's Film Adaptation classroom activity, complete taping and editing of your movie scene with your group. Individually, write a 1-page response about the process of adapting the scene in the novel to a script.

Day 5 - Discussion of Thought Questions

1. What do the reader learn about Madame Defarge's background in Book III, Chapters 10 and 12? What does this information and her subsequent actions reveal about her character?

Time:

7-10 minutes

Discussion:

In Chapter 10, Dr. Manette's letter of many years before is read aloud during Charles Darnay's second trial. In this letter, written during Manette's imprisonment in the Bastille, he tells a horrific story of egregious abuse and violence at the hands of the patriarch of the Evrémonde family. Also knowing that Charles Darnay is the son of this horribly immoral aristocrat, we can see the writing on the wall for the verdict in his trial, especially in a France that has become so bloodthirsty and unsparingly violent towards anyone even remotely associated with the aristocracy. Indeed, the jury convicts Darnay and sentences him to death in the next twenty-four hours. Then, in Chapter 12, Carton learns that Madame Defarge is actually that younger sister from Dr. Manette's story--the one who was whisked away by her brother to keep her safe--and so has an understandable personal grudge against the Evrémonde family. Carton also learns that Madame Defarge believes the revolution must eliminate all the aristocracy and their associates, while her husband believes in a more moderate approach. Betraying his profound sympathies for the revolutionaries' plight, Dickens makes clear that Madame Defarge's ruthless viciousness does not stem from an inherent character defect, but rather from all she has suffered in her life.

2. What does Madame Defarge's death reveal about her character? And what does

it foreshadow for the broader Revolution in France?

Time:

7-10 minutes

Discussion:

For Dickens, the French Revolution brought up many challenging issues, as he was a staunch political progressive himself who advocated for radical reforms of poor laws of the era and significant changes to England's approach to social inequity. *A Tale of Two Cities* demonstrates Dickens's conflicting feelings about the Revolution. He writes in great depth and detail about the poverty and oppression the French peasants suffered and vividly illustrates the callous barbarity of the aristocracy, suggesting that he understands the revolutionaries' motivations. At the same time, Dickens also unsparingly portrays the brutality of the revolutionaries' methods as they gain power and influence.

In many ways, Madame Defarge serves as both a character in her own right and a symbol for the broader motivations behind the Revolution. Early in the novel, Defarge seems mild and unthreatening, simply knitting quietly in the wine-shop. However, the reader soon learns that Defarge is knitting symbols into her shrouds-- symbols which serve as a register of names for all those people who Defarge wants to pay when the revolutionaries rise. This revelation betrays Defarge's true nature as a vengeful and blood-thirsty radical. As the revolution gets underway, Madame Defarge's true nature is revealed for all to see. She turns much of her passion for vicious retribution on Lucie Manette, cultivating an obsessive vendetta against Lucie and her loved ones and escalating her vindictive behavior towards the family as the novel proceeds and the French Revolution takes on its full force.

As mentioned previously, Dickens makes clear that he empathizes with the reasons behind Madame Defarge's bitter vendetta against the aristocracy. This suffering, as the reader learns later in the novel, was at the hands of the aristocracy, specifically the Evrémonde family, to which Charles Darnay is related by blood and Lucie Manette by marriage to Charles. Despite his sympathies however, Dickens stops short of showing support for Defarge's policy of retaliatory retribution against those who have harmed her and her family. In portraying Madame Defarge's death from her own gun's bullet, Dickens suggests that Defarge's passion for payback will eventually make her the oppressor of others, just as she was oppressed.

Finally, we see the reverberations of her death in the broader movement she represents, as Carton prophetically envisions all that will happen in the future to those he knows: Barsad, Cly, Defarge, the Vengeance, the Jury, and the Judge will all eventually be killed by the guillotine and the surrounding blood-thirsty culture they helped create; and Lucie and Darnay will live happily back in England, with all their future generations, including a son named after Carton himself, blessing his goodness and self-sacrifice. Clearly, Madame Defarge digs her own grave by sewing seeds of such hate and discord in the revolution she helped to start.

3. What is the thematic importance of Sydney Carton's ultimate sacrifice at the end of the novel? How does this event relate to prior instances of this theme (or these themes) earlier in the novel?

Time:

7-10 minutes

Discussion:

Many events happen in quick succession in the final chapters of *A Tale of Two Cities*, so as a reminder, in Book III, Chapter 13, Carton follows through in taking Darnay's place at his execution. After getting into the prison under false pretenses, Carton persuades Darnay to switch clothes with him and has him take a sleep-inducing sedative. Barsad comes in to take who he believes to be Carton out of the cell--in fact, Carton has stayed behind in Darnay's place and Darnay is now free. A jailer takes Carton to another room to await his execution. A woman there recognizes that he is not Darnay, but does not turn him in and instead asks to hold his "brave hand" as they are taken to the guillotine.

Finally in Chapter 15, Carton goes to his execution peacefully. He prophetically envisions all that will happen in the future to those he knows: Barsad, Cly, Defarge, the Vengeance, the Jury, and the Judge will all eventually be killed by the guillotine and the surrounding blood-thirsty culture they helped create; and Lucie and Darnay will live happily back in England, with all their future generations, including a son named after Carton himself, blessing his goodness and self-sacrifice. As he dies, he concludes, "It is a far, far better thing that I do than I have ever done; it is a far, far better rest than I go to than I have ever known." From the perspective of many readers and critics, Carton's ultimate sacrifice of his life for Darnay's strongly suggests a connection Jesus's crucifixion and subsequent resurrection in Christian religious teachings, which would have been very family to virtually all of Dickens's contemporaries.

Arising repeatedly throughout the novel, resurrection--both figuratively and literally--is one of the most important and overarching themes in *A Tale of Two Cities*. By far the most notable reference to resurrection in the novel relates to the complex relationship between Charles Darnay and Sydney Carton. Early in the novel, Carton's likeness to Darnay saves the latter from conviction and execution during his trial in England. Then again, at the end of the novel, their resemblance allows Carton to take Darnay's place just before his execution at the hands of the French revolutionaries. These instances of resurrection are laden with religious overtones, connecting Carton's willingness to sacrifice his life for Darnay to Christ's sacrifice for humanity on the cross.

In addition, related to the themes of Resurrection, Dickens focuses on the necessity of sacrifice to achieve happiness in *A Tale of Two Cities*. Again, this theme arises both for characters personally, as well as on a more communal and national level throughout the novel. On a societal level, for example, the French revolutionaries demonstrate that the shift towards a more equitable France requires the sacrifice of many different individuals and groups in the country. On a more personal level, when Charles Darnay is arrested again in Chapter 7 of Book the Third, the guard tells Manette to remember that state and societal interests should trump personal needs and loyalties. Madame Defarge makes a similar point to her husband when she is criticizing his loyalty to Manette, which she believes undermines Defarge's willingness to sacrifice for the revolutionary cause. Finally, Carton's willingness to sacrifice his own life for Darnay's not only allows the Darnay-Manette family to stay intact, but also facilitates Carton's own moral rebirth.

4. What do you think of the way that Dickens conveys the importance of family in the novel overall, and especially in Book III? How does this relate to events in his own life at the time?

Time:

7-10 minutes

Discussion:

A Tale of Two Cities focuses heavily on the importance of commitment to family, and this focus is especially reinforced in Book III of the novel. Dickens introduces this theme early on, with Lucie Manette's trip to rescue her father in Paris, although she has not seen him for most of her life. This theme continues to feature prominently throughout the novel, as Lucie and Charles Darnay struggle to keep their family intact over the course of the story. Indeed, when Darnay faces a death sentence, his primary concern is for his family and their loss. And, as a final reinforcement of the family ideal, Carton sacrifices his own family-less life for Darnay's, therefore facilitating the preservation of the Darnay and Manette families.

Interestingly, Dickens built *A Tale of Two Cities* around the stable romance and unfailing marriage between Charles Darnay and Lucie Manette--all while his own personal life was falling into disarray. For many years, Dickens had been locked in an unhappy union with Catherine Hogarth. But while he was acting in Wilkie Collins's play--incidentally, the inspiration for the seed idea of the novel--Dickens met and fell in love with a young actress named Ellen Ternan. His relationship with Ternan was the final nail in the coffin of his troubled marriage, causing him to his separation from Hogarth in 1859. Divorce, a rare occurrence at the time, was unsurprisingly strongly frowned upon in Victorian England. As a result, this highly publicized turn of events in Dickens's personal life, along with several subsequent affairs, which also garnered significant media attention, marred the famous author's previously wholesome reputation and towards the end of his life. All of these events going on in his personal life at the time undoubtedly influenced Dickens's writings on these topics and the way he envisioned the focus on family and marriage throughout the novel.

5. Having now read the end of the novel, what do you think of Carton's character development over the course of the novel? How does he change both his beliefs and actions as the novel proceeds? Why?

Time:

7-10 minutes

Discussion:

Although Sydney Carton initially appears to be a rather unsympathetic, boorish man, as the story progresses, Carton becomes one of the most surprising and dynamic characters in the novel. At the beginning, Carton is a London attorney who began his career with great potential, but has since devolved into a life of laziness, alcoholism, and vice. He believes his life is a waste and regularly makes a point to say that he does not truly care for anyone or anything. Yet despite his apparent apathy, the reader senses that Carton actually subconsciously longs for a greater sense of purpose and meaning in his life. Even early on in the novel, just after Carton has helped to rescue Charles Darnay from conviction and execution, Carton cynical and sarcastic comments about Lucie show both his bitter personal biases as well as revealing his secret, developing feelings for Lucie Manette. Over time, however, Carton comes to recognize his attraction towards Miss Manette. Although he initially dismisses his romantic feelings as completely unrealistic, he is eventually able to profess his love to her directly. Not surprisingly, Lucie goes on to marry Darnay anyway, and Carton persists in believing himself to be a worthless human being, but this scene marks a turning point in Carton's life.

Carton's ultimate sacrifice at the end of the novel--going to the guillotine in Darnay's place--has proven controversial for many readers and critics ever since *A Tale of Two Cities* was written. Some critics argue that this is the unavoidable (and unsurprising) conclusion of a novel that focuses so heavily on themes of sacrifice, redemption, and resurrection. In this reading of the story, Carton's sacrifice of his own life mimics Christ's sacrifice for humanity, giving new life to Charles Darnay through his own death. Dickens provides further reinforcement for this interpretation of the story through his frequent use of imagery generally associated with Jesus's crucifixion and resurrection, for example the references to wine and blood throughout the novel. Despite this symbolism and thematic repetition, other critics and readers argue that Carton's sacrifice is not necessarily all that meaningful, since he did not place a lot of value on his life in the first place. Although some readers may not see Carton's life and death as very significant, Dickens seems to suggest that Carton's self-sacrifice is a necessary part of giving his life meaning and purpose.

Day 5 - Short Answer Evaluation

1. Who does Cruncher recognize Solomon Pross as?

   _____

2. What does Cruncher reveal about Roger Cly?

   _____

3. What is Cruncher's unsavory secret profession?

   _____

4. Who is the third, previously unnamed accuser of Charles Darnay?

   _____

5. In what year did Dr. Manette write and hide the document?

   _____

6. In Dr. Manette's letter, what does the recently-assaulted woman keep repeating over and over again?

   _____

7. When Lucie faints after Darnay's trial, what does Carton do?

   _____

8. What do we learn is Madame Defarge's true identity?

   _____

9. Who switches places with Charles Darnay in prison?

10. Who kills Madame Defarge? How?

Answer Key

1. He recognizes him as the English spy, John Barsad.
2. That Roger Cly is not actually dead as everyone had thought.
3. Robbing graves.
4. Dr. Manette.
5. 1767.
6. She repeats the phrase "my husband, my father, and my brother!" and counts to twelve obsessively.
7. Carton carries Lucie out, whispers in her ear "A life you love," and kisses her.
8. Madame Defarge is actually that younger sister from Dr. Manette's story--the one who was whisked away by her brother to keep her safe--and so has an understandable personal grudge against the Evrémonde family.
9. Mr. Carton.
10. Miss Pross accidentally kills Madame Defarge with her own gun?

Day 5 - Crossword Puzzle

ACROSS

3. Loathing, disgust.
8. The Damay and Manette's final home.
10. Manete and Damay's daughter's name.
12. The traumatized woman counts to _____ obsessively.
14. Damay's third accuser.
15. Madame Defarge's killer.
17. Necktie.
18. Means of transport to the guillotine.
19. Persistence, obstinacy.
20. Hard to understand, mysterious.

DOWN

1. Degenerate or debaucherous person.
2. Amusing, strangely funny.
4. Menacing, foreboding.
5. Who takes Damay's place in prison?
6. Periodical which published novel (4 wds)
7. Solomon Pross is really _____ _____.
9. Someone's expression or face.
11. To hunt about, search around.
13. Wordy, verbose, talkative.
16. Cruncher reveals that _____ _____ isn't really dead.

Crossword Puzzle Answer Key

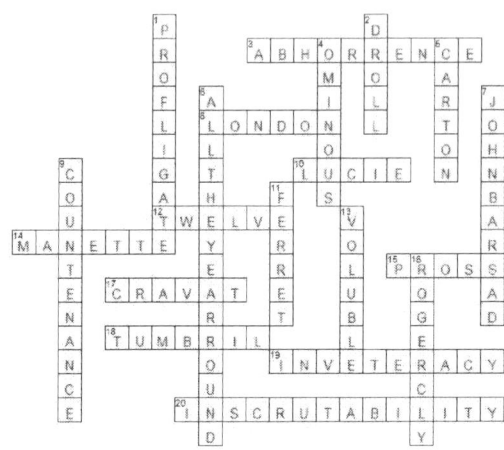

ACROSS

3. Loathing, disgust.
8. The Darnay and Manette's final home.
10. Manete and Darnay's daughter's name.
12. The traumatized woman counts to _____ obsessively.
14. Darnay's third accuser.
15. Madame Defarge's killer.
17. Necktie.
18. Means of transport to the guillotine.
19. Persistence, obstinacy.
20. Hard to understand, mysterious.

DOWN

1. Degenerate or debaucherous person.
2. Amusing, strangely funny.
4. Menacing, foreboding.
5. Who takes Darnay's place in prison?
6. Periodical which published novel (4 wds)
7. Solomon Pross is really _____ _____.
9. Someone's expression or face.
11. To hunt about, search around.
13. Wordy, verbose, talkative.
16. Cruncher reveals that _____ _____ isn't really dead.

Day 5 - Vocabulary Quiz

Terms

1. _____ abhorrence
2. _____ denunciation
3. _____ vaunting
4. _____ ferret
5. _____ countenance
6. _____ droll
7. _____ pinion
8. _____ inveteracy
9. _____ vestige
10. _____ ominous

Answers

A. To hold or tie someone's limbs.
B. Menacing, foreboding.
C. Persistence, obstinacy.
D. Publicly condemning or informing against someone.
E. Loathing, disgust.
F. Amusing, strangely funny.
G. Remainder, remnant.
H. Bragging, boasting.
I. To hunt about, search around.
J. Someone's expression or face.

Answer Key

1. E abhorrence: Loathing, disgust.
2. D denunciation: Publicly condemning or informing against someone.
3. H vaunting: Bragging, boasting.
4. I ferret: To hunt about, search around.
5. J countenance: Someone's expression or face.
6. F droll: Amusing, strangely funny.
7. A pinion: To hold or tie someone's limbs.
8. C inveteracy: Persistence, obstinacy.
9. G vestige: Remainder, remnant.
10. B ominous: Menacing, foreboding.

Day 5 - Classroom Activities

1. The Life and Times of Charles Dickens

Kind of Activity:

Long-term Project

Objective:

Students will conduct research on life in late 18th and early 19th century England, examine how specific societal changes may have impacted Dickens's life and writings, and present their research and findings to the class.

Common Core Standards:

CCSS.ELA-Literacy.CCRA.R.4, CCSS.ELA-Literacy.CCRA.R.5, CCSS.ELA-Literacy.CCRA.W.7, CCSS.ELA-Literacy.CCRA.W.8, CCSS.ELA-Literacy.CCRA.SL.4

Time:

20-25 minutes (recurring)

Structure:

For an overview of this unit-long project, see the description in Day #1.

For Day #5, if needed, review the purpose of the activity by reviewing how it will work and how it will continue through the unit. An overview of these review steps can be found in the Day #1-Day #4 descriptions of this activity's structure. These review steps can be skipped if they are unnecessary for your class at this stage.

In addition, for Day #5, introduce the expectations and stipulations for the final group presentation/project related to this activity. This presentation/project could take any form--digital/multimedia presentation, posters, performance, paper, etc.--but should include both evidence of a thorough and in-depth research in to the group's assigned theme, as well as in-depth analysis of at least 5 of the *A Tale of Two Cities* scenes studied in this unit. At this stage of this unit-long group project, groups should finalize the planning and development of their group presentation/project, so that it can be presented or submitted at the end of the unit.

After explaining the next steps related to the final presentation/project, as in previous days of this activity, the pre-assigned small groups continue to research their assigned theme--Science & Technology; Rebellions/Revolutions in the late 18th and early 19th centuries; Queen Victoria's reign; Dickens's Religious Worldview/ Outlook, Dickens's Literary & Philosophical influences; Literature in the Victorian era, Cultural/Religious Reactions to the French Revolution, etc.

Provide biographical sources on Dickens for students to read independently, or have them begin conducting their own research, depending on the time and resources available. These resources could include any of the following, in addition to many others:

Victorian England:

- http://www.english.uwosh.edu/roth/VictorianEngland.htm
- http://www.bbc.co.uk/history/british/victorians/
- http://www.aboutbritain.com/articles/victorian-era-1837-1901.asp
- https://www.wwnorton.com/college/english/nael/victorian/review/ summary.htm
- http://www.history.ac.uk/ihr/Focus/Victorians/article.html
- https://www.history.org.uk/resources/primary_resource_3871_134.html

Charles Dickens:

- http://www.biography.com/people/charles-dickens-9274087
- http://www.bbc.co.uk/history/historic_figures/dickens_charles.shtml
- http://www.online-literature.com/dickens/
- http://www.britannica.com/biography/Charles-Dickens-British-novelist
- http://www.dickens-online.info/charles-dickens-biography.htm
- http://www.pbs.org/wgbh/masterpiece/dickens/dickens.html
- http://charlesdickenspage.com/
- http://dickensmuseum.com/
- http://dickenslive.com/
- http://www.dickensfellowship.org/life-charles-dickens

A Tale of Two Cities Analysis:

- http://www.gradesaver.com/tale-of-two-cities
- http://www.novelguide.com/a-tale-of-two-cities/theme-analysis
- http://www.litcharts.com/lit/a-tale-of-two-cities/plot-overview
- http://www.online-literature.com/dickens/twocities/
- http://charlesdickenspage.com/cities.html
- http://www.pbs.org/wgbh/masterpiece/archive/110/110.html

As in Days #1-4, the group scribe should chart the sociological events related to their group's theme, with a particular eye toward the ways that Day 5's readings have expanded their understanding of their assigned theme. Next, each group will examine the day's readings to find textual examples of the assigned theme. The group will then analyze their selected pieces of textual evidence and add them to their overall analysis.

Finally, as in previous days, students will then share out one finding from their group with the whole class.

Ideas for Differentiated Instruction:

- Give students reading sections for research differentiated by reading level.
- Provide some groups with the option to read aloud the biographical section, or listen to/watch audio or video pieces about Dickens as a form of research.
- Assign students different roles—scribe, head researcher, lead note-taker, presenter, etc.—based on skills or areas for growth.
- Split students into groups by skill-set or areas of need, so that some groups can work more independently, and the teacher can support other groups more as needed.

Assessment Ideas:

- Student groups each generate a series of charts about an aspect of life or culture in Dickens's time and how it relates to his writings, with specific references to scenes from *A Tale of Two Cities*.
- Students present findings from group chart to the rest of the class.
- Students take notes, using an interactive handout (digital or paper), on other groups' theme presentations.
- Students present overall research and analysis at end of unit, using multimedia (audio/video/picture) presentations.

2. Making a Movie: Adapting "The Tale of Two Cities" for Film

Kind of Activity:

Performance

Objective:

Students will analyze the dramatic elements in various scenes in the novel, interpret the scenes into something that can be performed, create a film of the selected scene, and present their films to the class.

Common Core Standards:

CCSS.ELA-Literacy.CCRA.R.2, CCSS.ELA-Literacy.CCRA.R.4, CCSS.ELA-Literacy.CCRA.W.3, CCSS.ELA-Literacy.CCRA.SL.2

Time:

40-45 minutes

Structure:

Prior to class, select 4-5 short scenes from the novel that could be easily scripted and performed by small groups (of varying sizes).

Divide class into small groups of 4-5, depending on class size and number of individuals needed for each scene. Assign each group a scene (or have groups select their own scenes), and explain to the students that they will be reading their assigned/selected scene as a small group, turning it into a 5 minute scripted scene, filming their scene outside of class, and then presenting their short filmed scene to the class. Specify all students should have a speaking or acting role in the performance, but not all lines and passages written in each scene need to be included--it is up to the discretion of the group to include lines and interactions they think are most relevant to conveying the characters and story.

Give groups time to read the passages, prepare their scripts, and assign roles. After writing their scripts, give groups time to practice and prepare for filming.

Finally, have each of the groups film their scene separately, edit the film scene as a group, and then present their scene to the class.

Note: Depending on time, this activity can be split into multiple days. Alternatively, students can have sections of this activity assigned for homework over multiple days.

Ideas for Differentiated Instruction:

- Assign different roles to different students based on skill areas or areas for growth.
- Give students challenge/analysis questions to analyze about other groups performances.
- Provide some students with additional supports or assistance in preparing for their performance during the prep time (e.g. teacher will spend more time helping some groups brainstorm to devise the best approach).
- Assign different scenes (with different complexities and numbers of challenging vocabulary words) to different groups based on reading level.

Assessment Ideas:

- Students write a script based on the scene in the novel.
- Students film their scene as a group, edit it, and present the film to the class.
- Students complete and submit reflections on or assessments of other groups' films (qualitative or quantitative).
- After the performances, students can answer questions from others in the class about what choices they made about creating the mood (e.g. Why did you choose to include certain lines/characters in the scene and not others?)

3. Surprise Scene Workshop, Part 2: Creating Your Own Visualization of an "A Tale of Two Cities" Scene

Kind of Activity:

Artistic Response

Objective:

Students will evaluate the use of imagery and symbols in the etchings in Dickens's novel to convey larger themes, create their own etching or visual representation of their own scene from Part 1, and present their scene/visual representation to the class.

Common Core Standards:

CCSS.ELA-Literacy.CCRA.R.4, CCSS.ELA-Literacy.CCRA.R.7, CCSS.ELA-Literacy.CCRA.W.8, CCSS.ELA-Literacy.CCRA.W.9, CCSS.ELA-Literacy.CCRA.SL.1, CCSS.ELA-Literacy.CCRA.SL.5

Time:

30-35 minutes

Structure:

Throughout his writings, Dickens uses extensive imagery and evocative metaphors, allowing the reader to truly envision and experience the abstract themes he is trying to describe more concretely. In addition, he created his own elaborate etchings to further illustrate the themes and symbols he wants readers to envision and understand. In this activity, students will construct a creative representation of their own written poems (from the Classroom Activity from the previous day "Surprise Scene Workshop, Part 1: Writing Your Own "A Tale of Two Cities" Scene"), in whatever way they choose.

There can be limitations on the types of media students are allowed to use, or they can have free reign to choose whatever visual medium they want (e.g. collage, painting, drawing, mural, photography, computer-based graphic design, etc.). In addition, this project can be done individually or in small groups.

Lead students through a brief evaluation of the one of Dickens's scenes as connected to its etching. Examine one of the images, symbols, or themes Dickens references in the scene and the descriptions are conveyed visually in the etching. Have students supply a few examples of how they might choose to artistically represent a Dickens scene from a previous day in the unit or, alternatively, how they plan to visually portray their own scene.

Give students the remainder of the time to construct or complete their projects. Once the students' creative responses are complete, have students present their etchings to the class.

Ideas for Differentiated Instruction:

- Depending on student independence, assign them to work as individuals or in small groups.
- Split students into groups by skill-set or areas of need, so that some groups can work more independently, and the teacher can support other groups more (e.g. participating in the student discussion, helping to make connections, etc.).
- Assign different students or groups different poems to interpret, based on the poems' levels of complexity.
- Provide students with a variety of different means of artistically presenting their poems in order to give students of varying artistic abilities and preferences different ways to express themselves.

Assessment Ideas:

- Students present their artistic representation to the class and are graded (by the teacher or by peers) based on a rubric.
- Students offer feedback on other students' artistic representations, either in verbal or written form.
- Students write a 1-2 paragraph response about the artistic process of creating their piece.

Final Paper

Essay Questions

1. Select any two of the characters in *A Tale of Two Cities* and compare and contrast how these two characters approach and understand one of the themes or symbols in the novel.

2. Resurrection plays an important thematic role throughout many of the plot-lines in *A Tale of Two Cities*. Compare and contrast 2-3 examples of the theme of resurrection arising in different characters' lives. What role do these instances of resurrection take on in each different character's development and life? How does the frequent recurrence of this theme contribute to the overall message of the novel?

3. Based on your understanding of the tension between traditional/ conservative political ideologies and the growth of revolutionary movements in Dickens's time, as well as your knowledge of and additional external research about Dickens's own personal ideological beliefs and political views, write an analytical research paper about the way in which *A Tale of Two Cities* expresses the cultural shifts taking place in France and England during Dickens's time.

4. Choose one of the scenes in *A Tale of Two Cities* and re-write it from the perspective of a different character. Make sure to consider the unique voices, beliefs, and prejudices of both the original narrator of the scene, as well as those of the new scene narrator, and reflect those differences in your re-envisioning of the scene.

5. Based on your understanding of poverty, social injustice, and class struggles in late 18th and early 19th century England and France, as well as your knowledge of (and any research you choose to do about) Dickens's own personal beliefs around these subjects, discuss the portrayal of these themes in *A Tale of Two Cities*.

6. How does Dickens use the theme of Doubles & Duality in different ways over the course of *A Tale of Two Cities*? Examine how Dickens uses this theme throughout the novel to communicate different ideas about the story's characters and the world more broadly.

7. How does Dickens use the symbols of knitting and connective thread in different ways over the course of *A Tale of Two Cities*? Examine how these symbols are used in different contexts throughout the novel to communicate different ideas about the primary characters.

Advice on research sources

A. School or community library--Ask your reference librarian for help locating books on the following subjects:

* Charles Dickens and his biography

* Dickens's novels and other writings

* Late 18th and early-mid 19th century literature

* The late 18th and early 19th century and associated social and societal changes in England and surrounding countries

* Victorian literature, philosophies, and values

* Poverty and social justice issues in Victorian England

* Authors influenced by Dickens

B. Internet research

Victorian England:

- http://www.english.uwosh.edu/roth/VictorianEngland.htm
- http://www.bbc.co.uk/history/british/victorians/
- http://www.aboutbritain.com/articles/victorian-era-1837-1901.asp
- https://www.wwnorton.com/college/english/nael/victorian/review/summary.htm
- http://www.history.ac.uk/ihr/Focus/Victorians/article.html
- https://www.history.org.uk/resources/primary_resource_3871_134.html

Charles Dickens:

- http://www.biography.com/people/charles-dickens-9274087
- http://www.bbc.co.uk/history/historic_figures/dickens_charles.shtml
- http://www.online-literature.com/dickens/
- http://www.britannica.com/biography/Charles-Dickens-British-novelist
- http://www.dickens-online.info/charles-dickens-biography.htm
- http://www.pbs.org/wgbh/masterpiece/dickens/dickens.html
- http://charlesdickenspage.com/
- http://dickensmuseum.com/
- http://dickenslive.com/
- http://www.dickensfellowship.org/life-charles-dickens

A Tale of Two Cities Analysis:

- http://www.gradesaver.com/tale-of-two-cities
- http://www.novelguide.com/a-tale-of-two-cities/theme-analysis
- http://www.litcharts.com/lit/a-tale-of-two-cities/plot-overview
- http://www.online-literature.com/dickens/twocities/
- http://charlesdickenspage.com/cities.html
- http://www.pbs.org/wgbh/masterpiece/archive/110/110.html

The French Revolution:

- http://www.history.com/topics/french-revolution
- http://www.britannica.com/event/French-Revolution
- http://www.historytoday.com/maurice-cranston/french-revolution-ideas-and-ideologies
- http://www.eyewitnesstohistory.com/frenchrevolution.htm
- https://history.state.gov/milestones/1784-1800/french-rev
- https://www.youtube.com/watch?v=SyXcUMftRs8

Impact of the French Revolution in England:

- http://www.bl.uk/romantics-and-victorians/articles/the-impact-of-the-french-revolution-in-britain
- http://www.nationalarchives.gov.uk/pathways/citizenship/struggle_democracy/revolution.htm
- http://www.bbc.co.uk/history/british/empire_seapower/british_french_rev_01.shtml
- http://crossref-it.info/articles/178/impact-of-the-french-revolution
- http://www.historyhome.co.uk/c-eight/france/impactfr.htm

C. Personal experience
* What do you think about the importance of class and social status differences?
* What roles do class, social justice issues, and societal expectations play in your life?
* What are your perspectives on love, liberty, truth, power, class, honor, and human nature?
* Consider how Dickens's life experiences may have impacted his worldview and the perspectives portrayed in his writings, drawing upon examples in your own life of how your experiences have affected their outlooks about certain topics.

Grading rubric for essays

Style:

- words: spelling and diction
- sentences: grammar and punctuation
- paragraphs: organization
- essay: structure
- argument: rhetoric, reasonableness, creativity

Content:

- accuracy
- use of evidence
- use of research as appropriate
- addresses the question
- completeness
- uses literary concepts

Answer Key for Final Essays

Remember that essays about literature should not be graded with a cookie-cutter approach whereby specific words or ideas are required. See the grading rubric above for a variety of criteria to use in assessing answers to the essay questions. This answer key thus functions as a store of ideas for students who need additional guidance in framing their answers.

1. Select any two of the characters in *A Tale of Two Cities* and compare and contrast how these two characters approach and understand one of the themes or symbols in the novel.

Strong responses will include evidence of a close-reading of multiple specific and well-thought-out textual references, coupled with an evaluation of what these references suggest about the characters and how their unique voices develop the narrative. In addition, strong answers will clearly identify the subject matter, themes, or symbols the two characters contrast, and will select 1 focus theme or symbol to compare and contrast between the two characters' perspectives.

Finally, depending on the length of the essay, the best responses will include either a brief examination of how cultural and ideological debates in Dickens's time might relate to the comparative approaches the two characters take to their selected theme or symbol, or how these characters approaches to the subject matter relate to other characters' beliefs and ideologies in *A Tale of Two Cities*.

2. Resurrection plays an important thematic role throughout many of the plot-lines in *A Tale of Two Cities*. Compare and contrast 2-3 examples of the theme of resurrection arising in different characters' lives. What role do these instances of resurrection take on in each different character's development and life? How does the

frequent recurrence of this theme contribute to the overall message of the novel?

Due to the open-ended nature of this question, students could supply many possible well-supported and thoughtful answers. A strong response should include evidence of a close-reading of at least two events in the novel that feature resurrection (either somewhat literally or figuratively), as indicated by multiple specific and well-thought-out textual references, coupled with an evaluation of what each event or series of events suggests about the characters and their connection to the world around them.

Arising repeatedly throughout the novel, resurrection--both figuratively and literally--is one of the most important and overarching themes in *A Tale of Two Cities*. The first section of the novel is entitled "Recalled to Life," and is entirely focused on the rediscovery and rescue of Dr. Manette, who was thought to be dead but has actually imprisoned in the Bastille for eighteen years. The cryptic phrase "recalled to life" is the code for Mr. Lorry's and Lucie Manette's covert mission to Paris to rescue the Doctor. At one point, the phrase makes Mr. Lorry consider the ways in which being in prison as Doctor Manette was causes one to be disconnected from society for so long that it is almost as if one has died. This theme also comes up again (in a more humorous way) in the handling of Jerry Cruncher's unsavory side-job as a "Resurrection-Man"--a profession that deals primarily with grave-robbing and selling body parts for profit. Interestingly, despite the unpleasant nature of Cruncher's occupation, it leads him to the discovery of Roger Cly's empty grave--showing that the spy never actually died as everyone had thought. By far the most notable reference to resurrection in the novel relates to the complex relationship between Charles Darnay and Sydney Carton. Early in the novel, Carton's likeness to Darnay saves the latter from conviction and execution during his trial in England. Then again, at the end of the novel, their resemblance allows Carton to take Darnay's place just before his execution at the hands of the French revolutionaries. These instances of resurrection are laden with religious overtones, connecting Carton's willingness to sacrifice his life for Darnay to Christ's sacrifice for humanity on the cross.

3. Based on your understanding of the tension between traditional/conservative political ideologies and the growth of revolutionary movements in Dickens's time, as well as your knowledge of and additional external research about Dickens's own personal ideological beliefs and political views, write an analytical research paper about the way in which *A Tale of Two Cities* expresses the cultural shifts taking place in France and England during Dickens's time.

Strong answers will include 2-3 different textual examples from *A Tale of Two Cities* that demonstrate how Dickens incorporates and thinks about societal/ideological tensions in French (and British) society around the time of the French Revolution, and possibly more depending on the length of the essay. These examples should be carefully selected and analyzed in the context of Dickens's own personal beliefs and historical framework.

Finally, the best responses will include carefully chosen explanations of relevant sociological, political, and philosophical beliefs in late 18th and early 19th century French and British societies, as well as and a brief examination of how Dickens's life events might relate to the role of themes related to poverty and social justice in his writing.

4. Choose one of the scenes in *A Tale of Two Cities* and re-write it from the perspective of a different character. Make sure to consider the unique voices, beliefs, and prejudices of both the original narrator of the scene, as well as those of the new scene narrator, and reflect those differences in your re-envisioning of the scene.

All of the characters in *A Tale of Two Cities*--big and small alike--examine the same themes and symbols repeatedly throughout the novel. The characters either approach the themes from two different perspectives or, alternatively, from similar perspectives, but reaching different conclusions about how they should act and what these series of events reflect about human nature. Therefore, students can easily create strong, well-supported and thoughtful re-envisionings of scenes using any of the primary or secondary characters in the novel. For example, students could use the second courtroom scene, in which Darnay is unjustly convicted, and write the scene from the perspective of Madame or Monsieur Defarge or perhaps one of the Jacques.

Strong responses will include evidence of close-readings of the selected scene, demonstrated by insightful and relevant re-envisionings of the scene from the new character's perspective. In addition, strong answers will clearly identify the subject matter, themes, and symbols at play in the new interpretation of the scene. Students should also make sure to consider the unique voices, beliefs, and prejudices of both the original narrator of the scene, as well as the new scene narrator, and reflect those differences in their re-writes of the scene. Finally, depending on the length of the essay, the best responses will include the new narrator of the scene interacting with other characters in the novel, in order to demonstrate larger ideas that arise in the novel, outside of the one scene they are re-writing.

5. Based on your understanding of poverty, social injustice, and class struggles in late 18th and early 19th century England and France, as well as your knowledge of (and any research you choose to do about) Dickens's own personal beliefs around these subjects, discuss the portrayal of these themes in *A Tale of Two Cities*.

Unsurprisingly for a story that handles the French Revolution, class struggle is an overriding theme throughout the novel. Dickens clearly sympathizes with the motivations of the revolutionaries in France because of his own personal and political beliefs, which he demonstrates through his portrayal of the ruthlessness and cruelty of the aristocracy. Dickens clearly believes that there was significant justification for the peasants' desire for a societal overthrown. Ultimately however, despite his personal sympathies, Dickens ultimately sides with the argument against the Revolution, because of the overkill and bloodthirstiness of the revolutionaries as the movement gains more power. The novel also shows this transformation over the course of the story, demonstrating the evolution of the revolutionary movement from its focus on social justice and equality to a focus on retribution and revenge.

Furthermore, Dickens places significant emphasis throughout the story on the poverty and social injustice that the French lower classes had been struggling against leading up to the Revolution. Because of his own radical progressive politics, Dickens maintained complicated feelings about the French Revolution--while he ultimately did not support the revolutionaries' barbarous tactics, he sympathized with their motives. As mentioned previously, Dickens writes in great depth and detail about the poverty and oppression the French peasants suffered and vividly illustrates the callous barbarity of the aristocracy, showing that he understands the lower classes' desire to overthrow the ruling order of French society. Moreover, because of Dickens's commitment to progressive politics, plot-lines related to this theme come up in many of Dickens's novels, especially *Hard Times* and *Oliver Twist*.

Strong answers will include 2-3 different significant examples from the novel that demonstrate how Dickens incorporates and thinks about poverty- and social-justice-related elements and societal strictures, and possibly more depending on the length of the essay. These examples should be carefully selected and analyzed in the context of Dickens's historical framework. In addition, the best responses will include carefully chosen explanations of relevant ideological, philosophical, and political beliefs in late 18th and early 19th century French and British society, as well as and a brief examination of how Dickens's life events might relate to the role of faith-related themes in his writing.

6. How does Dickens use the theme of Doubles & Duality in different ways over the course of *A Tale of Two Cities*? Examine how Dickens uses this theme throughout the novel to communicate different ideas about the story's characters and the world more broadly.

Dickens introduces the theme of Doubles & Duality beginning with the very title of the novel, *A Tale of Two Cities*. Indeed, most of the characters and settings in the novel come in pairs--London/Paris and Darnay/Carton, just to name a few examples--and are played off each other throughout the novel. Another important aspect of this theme is the oppositional nature of many of these pairs. For example, Madame Defarge's shadowy appearance and dark demeanor notably contrasts with Lucie Manette's light physicality and the bright morality of her character. This theme of contrasting doubles even arises in the language Dickens chooses to use throughout the story, especially notable in the novel's famous opening: "It was the best of times, it was the worst of times, it was the age of wisdom, it was the age of foolishness...". Because of the prevalence of this theme throughout the novel, there are numerous examples students could use to support their own original argument about the importance of this theme in the overall plot.

Strong responses should include evidence of a close-reading of at least two different examples of doubles in *A Tale of Two Cities*. Particularly good responses to this topic will also demonstrate how these literal examples connect to the dualistic nature of man and the world and its implications in the story, employing direct textual references and original analysis of the importance of the similarities and differences between the use of these themes in the scenes or examples being examined. In addition, the strongest responses will include an examination of how Dickens's writing on this theme changes over the course of the novel. Although there are other strong ways to approach this essay question, a particularly good approach would include selecting one of the earlier references doubles and duality (e.g. Carton and Darnay's likeness of one another and its implications) and connecting this instance to the dualistic nature of good and evil and comparing it to later examples for analysis, examining how the two different scenes reflect different perspectives on or approaches to this theme. Finally, the best answers will examine and evaluate the implications and, if applicable, possible causes of any shifts in perspective that have taken place between the two (or more) scenes/examples.

7. How does Dickens use the symbols of knitting and connective thread in different ways over the course of *A Tale of Two Cities*? Examine how these symbols are used in different contexts throughout the novel to communicate different ideas about the primary characters.

Madame Defarge uses actual, physical symbols in her knitting to communicate with other members of the revolutionary movement (the symbols list names of those who would be condemned to death when the new revolutionary regime came to power). The knitting itself and the purpose behind it serves as a metaphor as well, however, of Madame Defarge's vengeful, malicious nature and, more broadly, the cunning and cold-blooded brutality of all the revolutionaries. Although Madame Defarge appears to be picture of calm, domestic femininity as she knits, she is actually sentencing her enemies to death. In a similar fashion, the impoverished and pitiable French peasants soon prove to be just as brutal and blindly violent as their former aristocratic oppressors. Significantly, Dickens's use of knitting imagery evokes the knitting and weaving traditionally associated with Fate in classical mythology, suggesting the inextricable link between vindictiveness and fate in the novel. Furthermore, Dickens's heavy reliance on this symbol suggests the timelessness of this tale throughout human history and the cyclical nature of fate and human destiny.

On the other side of the this symbolic duo, Lucie's golden blonde hair is emblematic of her magnetic beauty that attracts virtually every many she meets. Dickens uses her golden hair, however, to symbolize the goodness of her heart and how she binds her family together. He refers to her as "the golden thread" that keeps the family going. It is Lucie who connects Sydney Carton to Charles Darnay, Darnay to Doctor Manette, and Mr. Lorry to the family more broadly, and she is the motivation for many of the men in the story to pursue a greater purpose in their lives. Indeed, many of the characters give at least a passing thought to Lucie Manette's golden hair, suggesting that it has a symbolic power for many. For example, Jacques Three thinks about how much he'd like to see Lucie's golden hair on the guillotine's chopping block. Yet this will never come to pass, of course, as her hair also serves as something like a good luck charm for her and connects her to those she loves throughout the novel.

Strong responses should include a close reading of at least two (and probably 3-4) different references to knitting and thread in the novel, employing direct textual evidence and original analysis of the importance of the similarities and differences between the use of these themes in the scenes or examples being examined. In addition, the strongest responses will include an examination of how Dickens's writing on these themes changes over the course of the novel. Although there are other strong ways to approach this essay question, a particularly good approach would include selecting one of the earlier references to knitting and/or thread and comparing and contrasting it to later examples for analysis, examining how the two different scenes take different approaches to these symbols and reflect different meanings. Finally, the strongest answers will examine and evaluate the implications and, if applicable, possible causes of any shifts in perspective that have taken place between the two (or more) scenes/examples.

Final Exam

Multiple Choice

Circle the letter corresponding to the best answer.

1. In what year was Charles Dickens born?

    A. 1789
    B. 1859
    C. 1812
    D. 1800

2. Which of the following is NOT one of Charles Dickens's novels?

    A. Oliver Twist
    B. Northanger Abbey
    C. The Old Curiousity Shop
    D. The Pickwick Papers

3. For what was Dickens's father imprisoned when Dickens was 12 years old?

    A. Debt.
    B. Murder.
    C. Robbery.
    D. Evading Military Commission.

4. What is the title of Dickens's final, unfinished novel?

    A. "David Copperfield"
    B. "Bleak House"
    C. "Great Expectations"
    D. "The Mystery of Edwin Drood"

5. Where had Dr. Manette been imprisoned before the French Revolution?

    A. The Bastille.

B. La Force.
C. Versailles.
D. The Tower of London.

6. What is Charles Darnay initially put on trial for?

A. Grave robbing with Mr. Cruncher.
B. Stealing from Tellson's Bank.
C. Murder of John Barsad.
D. Traitorous activities (being a spy) against France.

7. What is the name of Lucie Manette's daughter?

A. Charlotte.
B. Lucie.
C. Therese.
D. Sydney.

8. What kind of shop does Monsieur Defarge and his wife own?

A. A cheese shop.
B. A wine shop.
C. A bakery.
D. A book shop.

9. Where does Mr. Lorry work?

A. Old Bailey.
B. The University.
C. The Tower of London.
D. Tellson's Bank.

10. Who is the witness against Charles Darnay in his original trial?

A. Mr. Stryver.
B. Mr. Carton.
C. Mr. Barsad.
D. Mr. Cruncher.

11. What is Jerry Cruncher's secret profession?

A. A hit man.
B. A spy.
C. A grave robber.
D. A wine maker.

12. What is the name of the neighborhood in which the Defarge's wine-shop is located and where much of the Paris action in the novel takes place?

A. Soho.
B. Saint Evrémonde.
C. Saint Antoine.
D. La Force.

13. After his re-arrest, how long is Charles Darnay imprisoned for?

A. One year and three months.
B. Five years.
C. Three weeks.
D. Two years and nine months.

14. What is the common French name that is shared by four members of the Defarge's revolutionary group?

A. Charles.
B. Jean.
C. Jacques.
D. Louis.

15. Why do Miss Pross and Jerry Cruncher shop at many different stores for food while the Darnays are in Paris?

A. There is a food shortage.
B. They are stealing food from the shops, so do not want to draw attention to themselves.
C. They are passing secret messages to shop owners.
D. They do not want to draw attention to their relative wealth.

16. Who is Roger Cly?

    A. One of Dr. Manette's fellow prisoners.
    B. One of Lucie Manette's suitors.
    C. A British spy.
    D. An associate of Mr. Lorry at Tellson's Bank.

17. What does Monsieur Defarge produce during Darnay's trial as evidence against him?

    A. An accussation written by John Barsad during his work with Charles Darnay as a spy.
    B. A confession written by Charles Darnay years earlier when he was allied with the Defarges.
    C. A document written by Dr. Manette during his imprisonment in the Bastille.
    D. An intercepted letter from Lucie to Darnay, which reveals his traitorous acts.

18. What is Charles Darnay's true identity?

    A. Miss Pross's brother, Solomon Pross.
    B. John Barsad, the English spy.
    C. The son of Monsieur and Madame Defarge.
    D. The son of the Marquis St. Evrémonde.

19. How does Charles Darnay avoid death at the end?

    A. Dr. Manette steps in and prevents Darnay from being executed.
    B. Lucie helps Darnay to escape from prison through the window bars.
    C. Sydney Carton pretends to be Darnay and is guillotined in his place.
    D. Madame Defarge recants her testimony and Charles Darnay is spared.

20. How was "A Tale of Two Cities" originally published?

    A. It was never published during Dickens's lifetime, but was instead discovered after Dickens's death.
    B. It was published as a daily column in The Times (the British newspaper).
    C. It was serialized (published in weekly segments) in Dickens's literary journal "All the Year Round."
    D. It was published as a full novel by Dickens's own publishing house.

Short Answer

1. Why did Dickens have to leave school at the age of 12? What did he do instead?

   _____

2. In what two cities is the novel primarily set?

   _____

3. What did Dr. Manette learn how to make in prison?

   _____

4. What major event is about to happen at the beginning of the novel?

   _____

5. What are the two charges against Charles Darnay at his two respective trials?

   _____

6. Where do the Defarge's hide their secret information for their revolutionary group?

   _____

7. How did the French revolutionaries prefer to execute those convicted in their tribunals?

   _____

8. How is Darnay able to avoid execution during his imprisonment at La Force?

   _____

9. How does Charles Darnay get acquitted in his first trial?

_____

10. Why does Madame Defarge have a particular grudge against Charles Darnay?

_____

Vocabulary Questions

Terms

1. _____ voluble
2. _____ protracted
3. _____ exordium
4. _____ potentate
5. _____ haggard
6. _____ apostrophise
7. _____ compunction
8. _____ penitential
9. _____ retainer
10. _____ abnegating

Answers

A. Related to penance or repentance.

B. Long and drawn out, prolonged.

C. Something that holds something else in place or together.

D. A leader or ruler, especially one who is totalitarian.

E. Looking exhausted or unwell, gaunt.

F. Rejecting or renouncing something cherished or valuable.

G. Introduction, beginning.

H. A digression or address to someone who is not present.

I. Wordy, verbose, talkative.

J. Guilt, misgivings, scruples.

Short Essays

1. Discuss the significance--symbolically, thematically, and narratively--of the opening paragraph of *A Tale of Two Cities*: "It was the best of times, it was the worst of times, it was the age of wisdom, it was the age of foolishness, it was the epoch of belief, it was the epoch of incredulity, it was the season of Light, it was the season of Darkness, it was the spring of hope, it was the winter of despair, we had everything before us, we had nothing before us, we were all going direct to Heaven, we were all going direct the other way--in short, the period was so far like the present period, that some of its noisiest authorities insisted on its being received, for good or for evil, in the superlative degree of comparison only."

_____

_____

_____

_____

_____

2. What is the significance of imprisonment, literally and symbolically, in *A Tale of Two Cities*?

_____

_____

_____

_____

_____

3. How does the theme of Family arise over the course of the novel? How does it relate to Dickens's experiences in his own life at the time?

_____

_____

_____

_____

Final Exam Answer Key

Multiple Choice

1. **(C)** 1812
2. **(B)** Northanger Abbey
3. **(A)** Debt.
4. **(D)** "The Mystery of Edwin Drood"
5. **(A)** The Bastille.
6. **(D)** Traitorous activities (being a spy) against France.
7. **(B)** Lucie.
8. **(B)** A wine shop.
9. **(D)** Tellson's Bank.
10. **(C)** Mr. Barsad.
11. **(C)** A grave robber.
12. **(C)** Saint Antoine.
13. **(A)** One year and three months.
14. **(C)** Jacques.
15. **(D)** They do not want to draw attention to their relative wealth.
16. **(C)** A British spy.
17. **(C)** A document written by Dr. Manette during his imprisonment in the Bastille.
18. **(D)** The son of the Marquis St. Evrémonde.
19. **(C)** Sydney Carton pretends to be Darnay and is guillotined in his place.
20. **(C)** It was serialized (published in weekly segments) in Dickens's literary journal "All the Year Round."

Short Answer

1. Dickens's father got into serious debt and had to go to debtor's prison. As a result, the family fell on hard times and Dickens had to leave school to go work in a blacking factory, in order to help support his family.
2. London and Paris.
3. Shoes.
4. The French Revolution.
5. In his first trial, Darnay is on trial for being an English spy. In his second trial, Darnay is on trial for being the son of a French aristocrat (and thus, part of the aristocracy).
6. Madame Defarge knits the information into shrouds, using symbols that only she can decipher.
7. The guillotine.
8. Dr. Manette uses his positive reputation among the revolutionaries, which he earns for having been imprisoned in the Bastille, to protect Darnay.

9. Sydney Carton, who looks very much like Mr. Darnay, presents himself, making positive identification of the defendant impossible.
10. Madame Defarge's true identity is the sister of the peasant girl who was raped and whose family was killed by Darnay's father.

Vocabulary Questions

1. I voluble: Wordy, verbose, talkative.
2. B protracted: Long and drawn out, prolonged.
3. G exordium: Introduction, beginning.
4. D potentate: A leader or ruler, especially one who is totalitarian.
5. E haggard: Looking exhausted or unwell, gaunt.
6. H apostrophise: A digression or address to someone who is not present.
7. J compunction: Guilt, misgivings, scruples.
8. A penitential: Related to penance or repentance.
9. C retainer: Something that holds something else in place or together.
10. F abnegating: Rejecting or renouncing something cherished or valuable.

Short Essays

1. The opening lines of *A Tale of Two Cities*--some of the most famous and iconic in the English language--reveal Dickens's own perspectives on the political and sociological changes happening leading up to the Revolution and during his own era. In addition, these lines relate to the cyclical sense of the past echoing into the future that Dickens hearkens back to so often over the course of the novel. In particular, these lines foreshadow the importance of three themes in the novel: Class Struggle, Inversions & Reversals, and Doubles & Duality.

    Unsurprisingly for a story that handles the French Revolution, class struggle is an overriding theme throughout the story, and is an important reference in this first paragraph of the novel. Dickens clearly sympathizes with the motivations of the revolutionaries in France because of his own personal and political beliefs, which he demonstrates through his portrayal of the ruthlessness and cruelty of the aristocracy. Dickens clearly believes that there was significant justification for the peasants' desire for a societal overthrown. Ultimately however, despite his personal sympathies, Dickens ultimately sides with the argument against the Revolution, because of the overkill and bloodthirstiness of the revolutionaries as the movement gains more power. The novel also shows this transformation over the course of the story, demonstrating the evolution of the revolutionary movement from its focus on social justice and equality to a focus on retribution and revenge.

Second, relating to the novel's focus on Class Struggle, the theme of Inversions & Reversals is also an inevitable result of story surrounding a sociological event like the French Revolution. And, these first lines suggest the importance this theme will take on over the course of the story. This Revolution completely mixed up French society and turned all of the societal norms on their heads. For example, upon his return to France, Darnay notes that in the new social order, noblemen are in prison with outlaws as their judges, juries, and executioners. This revolutionary society, however, allows for Carton to replace Darnay before the latter's execution--showing that in a system that has been turned so upside-down, a bad man can also take a good man's place.

Finally, a third overarching aspect of the novel that is introduced in these opening lines is the theme of Doubles & Duality. Dickens introduces this theme beginning with the very title of the novel, *A Tale of Two Cities.* Indeed, most of the characters and settings in the novel come in pairs-- London/Paris and Darnay/Carton, just to name a few examples--and are played off each other throughout the novel. Another important aspect of this theme is the oppositional nature of many of these pairs. For example, Madame Defarge's shadowy appearance and dark demeanor notably contrasts with Lucie Manette's light physicality and the bright morality of her character. This theme of contrasting doubles is reflected in the first paragraph of the novel, and the theme arises again and again throughout the novel.

2. More like a motif than an explicit symbol, the frequent occurrence of different forms of imprisonment in the novel serves as a symbol for the ways many of the different characters experience confinement, captivity, and isolation in their lives. Both Dr. Manette and Charles Darnay experience literal physical imprisonment in French fortresses, which reflects the over-arching importance of social inequality and political upheaval as narrative components in *A Tale of Two Cities.*

Yet, as the novel demonstrates, for many characters, including Manette and Madame Defarge, the memories of past bad experiences prove to be just as limiting and imprisoning as actually being in jail. These more symbolic forms of imprisonment and the ways in which they haunt characters throughout the novel hearkens back to another theme of the novel: Inversions & Reversals. Finally, for a character like Sydney Carton, his own choices in life have created a prison of his own making in which he feels his existence is meaningless--therefore, he is only able to break out of the "prison" of the life he has created, by sacrificing his own worthless life (in his eyes) for that of an admirable man like Darnay. This final example of symbolic imprisonment relates to yet another important theme in the novel: the necessity of sacrifice as a means of achieving salvation.

3. The focus on Family--more specifically, the focus on maintaining the family unit and the importance of sacrificing for one's family--is a

recurrent theme throughout *A Tale of Two Cities*. This focus on the importance of commitment to family is interesting, considering the events happening in Dickens's personal life at the time he was writing the novel. Dickens introduces this theme early on, with Lucie Manette's trip to rescue her father in Paris, although she has not seen him for most of her life. This theme continues to feature prominently throughout the novel, as Lucie and Charles Darnay struggle to keep their family intact over the course of the story. Indeed, when Darnay faces a death sentence, his primary concern is for his family and their loss. And, as a final reinforcement of the family ideal, Carton sacrifices his own family-less life for Darnay's, therefore facilitating the preservation of the Darnay and Manette families.

Interestingly, Dickens built *A Tale of Two Cities* around the stable romance and unfailing marriage between Charles and Lucie--all while his own personal life was falling into disarray. For many years, Dickens had been locked in an unhappy union with Catherine Hogarth. But while he was acting in Wilkie Collins's play--incidentally, the inspiration for the seed idea of the novel--Dickens met and fell in love with a young actress named Ellen Ternan. His relationship with Ternan was the final nail in the coffin of his troubled marriage, causing him to his separation from Hogarth in 1859. Divorce, a rare occurrence at the time, was unsurprisingly strongly frowned upon in Victorian England. As a result, this highly publicized turn of events in Dickens's personal life, along with several subsequent affairs, which also garnered significant media attention, marred the famous author's previously wholesome reputation and towards the end of his life.

Final Exam Answer Key

GradeSaver™

Getting you the grade since 1999™

Other Lesson Plans from GradeSaver™

12 Angry Men
1984
A Christmas Carol
A Doll's House
Alice in Wonderland
Allen Ginsberg's
  Poetry
All Quiet on the
  Western Front
Animal Farm
An Inspector Calls
Antigone
A Separate Peace
A Streetcar Named
  Desire
A Tale of Two Cities
A Thousand
  Splendid Suns
Atonement
Beowulf
Brave New World
Call of the Wild
Catching Fire

Cat's Cradle
Death of a Salesman
Do Androids Dream
  of Electric Sheep?
Doctor Faustus
  (Marlowe)
Dubliners
Emily Dickinson's
  Collected Poems
Esperanza Rising
Everyman: Morality
  Play
Fahrenheit 451
Flannery O'Connor's
  Stories
Flowers for
  Algernon
Frankenstein
Great Expectations
Gulliver's Travels
Hamlet
Heart of Darkness

House on Mango
  Street
In Cold Blood
In the Time of the
  Butterflies
Into the Wild
Jane Eyre
John Donne: Poems
Julius Caesar
Kate Chopin's Short
  Stories
Leaves of Grass
Life of Pi
Looking for Alaska
Lord Byron's Poems
Lord of the Flies
Macbeth
Master Harold...
  And the Boys
MAUS
Medea
Merchant of Venice
Middlesex

For our full list of over 300 Study Guides, Quizzes, Lesson Plans
Sample College Application Essays, Literature Essays and E-texts, visit:

www.gradesaver.com

GrAdeSaver™

Getting you the grade since 1999™

Other Lesson Plans from GradeSaver™

Mockingjay

Mythology

Never Let Me Go

Night

Oedipus Rex or
Oedipus the King

Of Mice and Men

Oliver Twist

One Flew Over the
Cuckoo's Nest

Oroonoko

Oryx and Crake

Othello

Our Town

Paper Towns

Persepolis: The
Story of a
Childhood

Poe's Poetry

Pride and Prejudice

Purple Hibiscus

Rip Van Winkle and
Other Stories

Robert Frost: Poems

Robinson Crusoe

Roll of Thunder,
Hear My Cry

Romeo and Juliet

Rosencrantz and
Guildenstern Are
Dead

Shakespeare's
Sonnets

Short Stories of
Ernest
Hemingway

Siddhartha

Songs of Innocence
and of Experience

Tess of the
D'Urbervilles

The Adventures of
Huckleberry Finn

The Adventures of
Tom Sawyer

The Alchemist
(Coelho)

The Bloody
Chamber

The Book Thief

The Brief Wondrous
Life of Oscar Wao

The Canterbury
Tales

The Catcher in the
Rye

The Color Purple

The Count of Monte
Cristo

The Crucible

The Curious
Incident of the
Dog in the Night-
time

The Diary of a
Young Girl by
Anne Frank

For our full list of over 300 Study Guides, Quizzes, Lesson Plans
Sample College Application Essays, Literature Essays and E-texts, visit:

www.gradesaver.com

GradeSaver™

Getting you the grade since 1999™

Other Lesson Plans from GradeSaver™

The Fault in Our
  Stars
The Giver
The God of Small
  Things
The Grapes of Wrath
The Great Gatsby
The Guest
The Handmaid's
  Tale
The Hobbit
The Hot Zone
The Hunger Games
The Jungle
The Kite Runner
The Legend of
  Sleepy Hollow
The Love Song of J.
  Alfred Prufrock

The Martian
  Chronicles
The Maze Runner
The Metamorphosis
The Namesake
The Odyssey
The Old Man and
  the Sea
The Outsiders
The Pearl
The Rime of the
  Ancient Mariner
The Road
The Scarlet Letter
The Story of My
  Life
The Stranger
The Things They
  Carried
The Tortilla Curtain

The Waste Land
The Yellow
  Wallpaper
Things Fall Apart
Thirteen Reasons
  Why
To Build a Fire
To Kill a
  Mockingbird
Touching Spirit Bear
Trifles
Uncle Tom's Cabin
Wordsworth's
  Poetical Works
Wuthering Heights
Young Goodman
  Brown and Other
  Hawthorne Short
  Stories

Made in the USA
Lexington, KY
26 February 2018